A Fool's Gold

By the same author

Where the Rivers Ran Backward

A Fool's Gold

A Story of Ancient Spanish Treasure, Two Pounds of Pot,
and the Young Lawyer Almost Left Holding the Bag

Bill Merritt

BLOOMSBURY

Author's note: This book isn't journalism. It is filled with made-up individuals, composite characters, and descriptions that do not match anything in the real world. If you think something in here is about you, it isn't. And, if you think you are going to make a big deal out of it, I've got plenty more on you that doesn't appear in the book, so think again.

Published by Bloomsbury Publishing, New York and London
Distributed to the trade by Holtzbrinck Publishers

All papers used by Bloomsbury Publishing are natural, recyclable products made from wood grown in well-managed forests.
The manufacturing processes conform to the environmental regulations of the country of origin.

Library of Congress Cataloging-in-Publication Data

Merritt, William E.
A fool's gold : a story of ancient Spanish treasure, two pounds of pot, and the young lawyer almost left holding the bag / William Merritt.—1st U.S. ed.
p. cm.
ISBN-13: 978-1-59691-099-7 (hardcover)
ISBN-10: 1-59691-099-2 (hardcover)
1. Lawyers—Oregon—Biography. 2. Law—Oregon—Anecdotes. I. Title.

KF373.M463A3 2006
340'.092—dc22
2005015770

First U.S. Edition 2006

1 3 5 7 9 10 8 6 4 2

Typeset by Palimpsest Book Production Limited,
Polmont, Stirlingshire, Scotland
Printed in the United States of America by
Quebecor World Fairfield

To Wesley with the adventuring heart. May you see all the things you hope to see, and discover others you never dreamed of. May your dreams pale in comparison to the life you live, and may you return home with lots of pictures.

OREGON NAMES

THE OREGON HIGHWAY Department used to have a sign at the foot of Neahkahnie Mountain that spelled the name phonetically: NEE-A-KAH-NEE.

They don't seem to do that anymore out of what, I suppose, is an attempt to protect the feelings of Indians by not reducing their linguistic heritage to roadside baby-talk. So, now, the only signs that spell names phonetically are on reservations, where the Indians aren't nearly as squeamish.

Oregon names are confusing because they tend to be pronounced the way a child would sound them out. It takes new residents a while to get the hang of this. Nobody east of the Rockies, for example, seems to know how to say the name of the state, stressing, as they do, the last syllable, to produce the discordant *or-ree-GONE* in place of the lovely *ORE-ri-gun* we who live here use.

Grady Jackson, a client I had for a few months over on the Coast, once told me, "You've got to pronounce Oregon names like you're just learning to read." I was fairly new to the state, then, and he had caught me trying to pronounce *Yaquina* with a hard *q* and an elongated, French kind of *ee* in place of the *i*. "*Yuh-KWIN-a,*" he said. "Just like it's spelled." He had a theory about that, just as he had a theory about most things.

"Meriwether Lewis was a big, educated deal. He went to balls at the White House and hung out with the French ambassador, and when he came out here, he gave our rivers fancy, French names like *Willamette*. Now I don't mean this as a criticism of nineteenth-century

1

public education, but the settlers didn't travel all the way across the continent because they got good grades in French.

"When they showed up out here, they held Mr. Meriwether Lewis's map up to the light and turned it this way, and that, until they had the words facin' the right direction. Then they puzzled over the spelling, trying out one thing and another, until they fetched up on *wuh-LAM-ut*. And, no matter what Mr. Meriwether Lewis may have had in mind, *wuh-LAM-ut* it has stayed ever since."

Grady may have been onto something. Like most things he told me, it was hard to tell how much truth there was to it. I'm not clear why it would even apply to Indian names, but I do know I would never have come up with *NEE-A-KAH-NEE* on my own.

1

GRADY JACKSON DIDN'T scare worth a damn—which meant he got to live his life pretty much any way he pleased, even if the rest of us had trouble deciphering his motives.

By the time I met him, he was famous on the Oregon Coast for lots of things, including winning the Distinguished Service Cross on Guadalcanal. That had something to do with pig latin and being surrounded by Japanese soldiers—I had to wait until his funeral before I got the story straight. But what Grady was most famous for was being the Crazy Man of Neahkahnie Mountain.

It was easy to see how he had gotten the reputation. He spent the last ten years of his life telling everybody within earshot about strange, marked rocks, and chests filled with gold that only he knew how to find. And he *would* find, too, just as soon as the State of Oregon let him back onto the beach to dig them up—which is where the law firm of Thaddeus Silk & Assoc. came in. Paying lawyers to get permission to dig holes in a state beach seemed like an expensive way to go crazy to me, but Grady was a grown man, and as long as he had the money, Thaddeus, and then I, were more than willing to provide all the legal help he needed.

With any luck, the lawsuits could have gone on forever. When Grady got a thing into his head, it didn't come back out again. In 1940, he had been in basic training at Ft. Campbell when he'd got it into his head he wasn't going to make his bed.

"Woman's work," he told the drill sergeant. Grady might even have believed it. He was from Flat Lick, Kentucky, which sounds like the kind of place women make beds.

His drill sergeant didn't care much about reasons. He did what drill sergeants do and stood Grady at the foot of his bed, leaned into his face, and informed Private Jackson that he was going to get his ass in gear and straighten out that piece-of-shit bunk of his, NOW, Dick Brain.

And Grady did what Grady did. He said, "Woman's work."

Oddly, Grady didn't seem to mind doing all sorts of other things women do. He cheerfully mopped the floor. He washed pots in the mess hall. He sewed patches on his uniform. He scrubbed windows. But he wouldn't make his bed.

That morning, he stayed behind to work on his bed while everybody else marched off to breakfast. When everybody else came marching back, there was Private Jackson looking like trooper-of-the-month in his smartly tucked fatigues, spit-shined combat boots, and glittering brass. Only, he was a trooper-of-the-month with an unmade bunk.

From then on, the entire platoon was confined to barracks—at least as far as weekend passes and trips to the commissary and the enlisted men's club were concerned. As far as forced marches and extra physical training were concerned, they weren't confined anywhere. But that didn't work, either—at least not the way it was supposed to. The platoon didn't turn against Grady. They admired him. Grady could shoot the eye out of a gnat at four hundred meters. He could break down and reassemble an M1 carbine in less time than it took to name the parts. He was generous about helping the other guys get acquainted with their own rifles, and before long, his bed started showing up made—as crisp as any bunk anywhere.

The platoon went back to having weekend passes and beers at the enlisted men's club, and a normal schedule of marches and physical training, until the morning the drill sergeant caught a trooper from Louisville in mid–hospital corner, making Grady's bunk. That evening, while the rest of the platoon was cleaning the latrine with toothbrushes, the drill sergeant took Grady out for some individual training.

Traditionally, individual training involved fists, but, in Grady's case,

4

the drill sergeant thought there might be a better way. Grady was a big, strong mountain boy, and there are no guarantees in a fistfight. Instead, he loaded Grady with a full combat pack, a rifle, and a helmet, and the two set out for the rifle range at a dead run.

The drill sergeant should have chosen fists. With the run, he was lucky to make it back alive. Even loaded down with a combat pack, a rifle, and a steel pot bouncing on his head, that mountain boy could run a drill sergeant into the ground. And, come morning, there he was again, at the foot of his unmade bunk, saying, "Woman's work." He said the same thing in the stockade the next day.

The guards were even more single-minded than the drill sergeant. But, they could never get him to make his bed. After a while, other prisoners began talking about woman's work, too, and the previously tidy stockade was threatening to take on the disheveled look of a college dorm. For the sake of an orderly administration of the Ft. Campbell prison system, it was back to the platoon for Grady Jackson, and the trooper from Louisville found himself officially assigned to make Grady's bed.

A tenacious litigant can be the bread and butter and marmalade of anybody's law practice, and when it came to suing the state to let him dig for lost treasure on Neahkahnie Beach, Grady wasn't ever going to quit. Except for being crazy, he was the ideal client. I inherited him when Thaddeus died.

Thaddeus had believed in luck. "I hired you because you're lucky," he told me. "Some lawyers are lucky, and some aren't. Myself, I'm not much good at luck, so I have to get people like you working for me and let the good fortune trickle uphill."

Trying to piggyback off somebody else's luck was as much of a guiding principle as Thaddeus ever seemed to aspire to. But, it didn't work out. The morning after he told me that, Sophie found him dead next to his desk. That was in the spring of 1981.

2

I WAS LATE for work that day. When I finally did roll in, I had trouble getting into the office. The fact was, I had trouble getting off the elevator. The hall was packed with secretaries and receptionists from other floors trying to see what was happening.

The police were already inside, and so were television crews. Sophie was there, too, and Tail Pipe, and Thaddeus's secretary, Jolene, was at the front desk reading a biography of Benito Mussolini. Behind her, a pair of investigators from the Bar Association with serious, we-mean-business looks on their faces, were rummaging through files. Somehow the bar had gotten a court order freezing what little was left in Thaddeus's trust account the moment Sophie dialed 911.

The police felt intruded on by the Bar Association. "What do you bet"—a tall cop smiled a knowing smile at a sweet-looking, blond policewoman—"the judge who signed that order is a member of the bar himself?"

The blond policewoman gave the tall cop a puzzled look, then turned back to trying to keep the news crews from trampling any more evidence. In the middle of it all, Sophie was bellowing that Thaddeus had been murdered.

"They *scared* him to death," she wailed. "They snuck in when he was alone and . . . and . . . Everybody knew Thaddie had a weak heart. Here." She thrust a sheaf of medical documents into the hands of a hungover-looking female reporter from *Newsroom 7*. "You can see for yourself how weak his heart was."

The reporter stared at the papers, not quite knowing what to think about them. But she knew what to think about Sophie.

Ratings.

The reporter shoved her microphone into Sophie's face, then nodded expectantly while the newly bereaved sister psychobabbled paranoia to a waiting city.

"He was working late and they snuck in to steal the treasure and . . . and when he wouldn't give it to them, I . . . I . . ." Sophie broke down, and the reporter glanced at the camera crew to make sure they had it on tape for their six-o'clock news show.

Sophie was on the wrong side of sixty, but she was still an ornate woman. Leopard-spot prints were her signature fabric. She sported tight skirts, tighter blouses, and enough metal jewelry to put her in real danger in a lightning storm. She had big, blond hair, and an even bigger voice left over from twenty years in the Marine Corps. And she was family, so Thaddeus hadn't had any choice but to let her move into the spare bedroom after his wife died.

Sophie yelled and bullied her way through life with a gusto and a lack of judgment that made everyone who came within range wonder why Thaddeus hadn't already had another heart attack. We all knew he was heading for one.

He may even have been counting on it. But that didn't mean he wasn't an excellent candidate for murder, too. By the time he hired me, he had cut so many corners he was living entirely among the curves. Even for a criminal-defense attorney, Thaddeus Silk had accumulated an ungainly roster of people who would have loved to do him in.

I wasn't one, though. I liked Thaddeus. He was a gentle, rumpled old man in a pleasant, out-of-date tweed suit. He kept a messy desk and a messier office, and he spoke quietly in a thoughtful sort of way. Most of all, there was no rosewood or brass in his office, which made him seem honest and down-to-earth compared to the other lawyers I knew. And he had given me a job.

I didn't find out about the investigations from the Bar Association until after I went to work for him. Or the trust accounts or the extra sets of ledgers. Or the clients he had left standing alone in court. Or the times he'd showed up at the wrong place with the wrong documents. Or the cases he had forgotten about entirely. But no matter what a hair-raising mess he'd made of his professional life, going to work must have seemed easy and restful compared to what he faced at home. It was no wonder he had sought the consolation of quieter women. Unfortunately for Thaddeus, he had been consoling himself with a quieter woman the night he'd had his first heart attack.

Whatever else you might say about Sophie, she'd kept her nose out of Thaddeus's professional life, at least until the evening the call came from the secret love nest telling her that her brother was on the way to the emergency room. Sophie wasn't carrying a torch for the memory of Thaddeus's wife. She hadn't even liked her much while she was alive. But the idea of a bimbo in a secret love nest—well, it just wasn't seemly. A respected member of the legal community had to keep up appearances, and Sophie set out to make sure Thaddeus kept up his.

When he recovered enough to come back to work, he took one look at the big, steel desk she had installed in the reception area while he was still in intensive care, grabbed his chest, sat heavily on one of the chairs he kept for clients, and breathed deeply for a few minutes. Then he drove himself up to the Oregon Health Sciences University to have his heart monitored. He knew exactly what that desk meant. Thaddeus Silk & Assoc. had a new office manager.

With Sophie out front managing his law practice, Thaddeus spent most of the time in his office with the door closed. It may have helped his peace of mind, but the idea of Thaddeus Silk's doing legal work outside the sight of others did not raise anybody else's comfort level.

He still kept away from home as much as he could, but his nights at the secret love nest were over. Most evenings, he stayed late at the office where Sophie could find him. Usually, he went home afterward, but sometimes, he drove up to the hospital. On nights when Sophie couldn't reach him at work, she would launch a surprise inspection at OHSU, and there Thaddeus would be, his heart connected to a machine.

That last night when Sophie couldn't find him at the hospital, she had phoned every woman she knew. That took a lot of phoning, and some of the women hadn't been friendly about it. And those who started out friendly, well, the friendliness didn't last once Sophie started calling them sluts and demanding they put Thaddie on the phone this very minute before I come over and snatch him out of there myself.

About six in the morning, she ran out of women to threaten, climbed into the car, and drove to the office. Clues to whomever Thaddeus was hosing were bound to be around there, somewhere. That's when she found him crumpled into a pile of files next to his desk and called 911 and the television stations. I never discovered which number she dialed first.

The office had been ransacked. At least the police thought it had. I thought it was hard to tell. Sometimes burglars leave places looking the way that office looked. But, so did Thaddeus.

At first glance, it didn't look much different from the way his office always looked. Files he might actually have worked on sometime were scattered in heaps on the carpet. More files were spilling off his desk. His credenza was jumbled with legal documents and law books that had vanished from the courthouse so long ago the librarian had given up looking for them. In the corner by the window, half-buried under yet more files, was an old-fashioned black floor-safe with faded, gold letters, a spin dial, and a steel handle. The letters spelled out R RICH & CO, which Jolene said was the name of one of Thaddeus's clients who had disappeared into the prison system and never reemerged.

When I looked closely, though, the police may have been right. It did seem as if drawers were open that usually weren't, and files were strewn about that I had last seen in cabinets. So, maybe, somebody had gone through Thaddeus's office.

"We'll need a complete inventory," one of the investigators from the bar said, smirking at the mess. "You *are* the associate, aren't you?" He was about forty, with the waxen, kept-away-from-the-sun look of the Undead in old vampire movies.

I nodded, gloomily. It had just become my job to go through those files, figure out what the legal issues were, what needed to be done, what had already been done, what Thaddeus had forgotten to do, and then prepare a report on it for the Bar Association. Then I was going to have to call each of Thaddeus's clients and update them on their cases. I wasn't looking forward to any of that.

"Don't make us wait too long." The investigator from the bar handed me his card so I would know where to call when the inventory was ready. He was having trouble suppressing a grin.

The police interviewed Sophie and wrote down what she said. But I don't think they ever took that murder business seriously. I think they'd been wanting to get inside Thaddeus's offices for a long time, and all the yelling about murder had given them the excuse they needed to search the place without a warrant. Whatever. Portland's finest began popping odds and ends from Thaddeus's life into plastic freezer bags.

Getting into the safe didn't turn out to be much of a problem. Thaddeus hadn't been any more careful with the combination than he had with anything else in his professional life. The police made a little ceremony out of opening it.

A drug-sniffing Labrador sat in front of the safe with the look of a dog who knew his duty and was doing it, his nose no more than six inches from the dial. A police photographer set up his camera. Sophie took out a big flash camera of her own. Jolene stood at the ready with her notary stamp and a piece of paper, while the rest of us crowded in a semicircle to get the first glimpse inside.

I don't know what the cops expected. Sophie was sure Spanish gold was in there. The people from the bar were hoping for wads of cash. The money from Thaddeus's trust account had to have gone somewhere. I was pretty sure the one thing Thaddeus did not have was wads of cash. Watching him juggle his affairs over the past three months had been a study in how not to make ends meet. I was right about that, too. Or, almost right.

There turned out to be one, single wad of cash: a stack of twenties totaling $4,980. That seemed like an unlikely amount to me, and my guess is that Thaddeus had needed money one day, reached in, helped himself to a Jackson, and drawn the total down from the $5,000 he'd started with.

The twenties must have been there a while, too. They were all at least eleven years old—series 1970 and earlier. I was surprised Thaddeus had gone that long and only dipped in once. It seemed un-Thaddeus-like, somehow.

A .22-caliber pistol was in the safe, along with ten boxes of ammunition, half a bottle of Old Grand-Dad, a Hamilton railroad watch, and a wedding ring with the name of Thaddeus's wife inscribed inside. There was also a cigar box with three passports, and eleven driver's licenses from six different states, each with Thaddeus's picture. But the names weren't his. We had found his escape kit, in case the big heart attack took too long to save him from the rest of his troubles.

The police popped the passports and driver's licenses and the pistol into freezer bags. For good measure, they popped the twenties into a freezer bag, too, and took them all away.

And that was it. No ancient Spanish treasure at all—which set Sophie off on another cataclysm of wailing. She demanded the police do something right *now* before she had their badges. Then she noticed a curious thing. "There's a streak in there. A gold streak."

There was, too. When we looked, we could see a broad, metallic-looking streak along the inside of the safe, as if something gold-colored had scraped the wall.

By then, the police were fed up with Sophie and didn't care enough about that streak to take a sample. But she set them straight, and the tall cop pulled out a penknife and flaked a few bits of gold into an envelope.

I wasn't persuaded it was gold, but Jolene knew better. After the police left, she explained about malleability, and how gold is the only metal that can be hammer-welded, and because it's so soft, if there's a metallic streak on the inside of an iron safe, then most likely it is gold. She was right, too. When the report came back, the flakes were almost pure gold.

That's the kind of thing Jolene would have known. Nobody was better educated, in a self-educated sort of way. In fact, she spent most of her time at Thaddeus Silk & Assoc. reading quietly at her desk.

Working for Thaddeus had been a good fit for Jolene. Any other place, she would have been out the door, busted from the work-release program that had brought her to Thaddeus, and back in the can, but as Thaddeus had once told me, "The thing about cheating on your taxes is, you can never fire your secretary."

3

JOLENE HADN'T STARTED out as a secretary. She had come on board with the grand title of director of marketing, and the mandate to bring in enough new retainers to meet her own paycheck and everybody else's. Which is why she'd hit on the idea of an ad in the yellow pages. A full-page ad in the yellow pages, she told Thaddeus, would be just the ticket to reach out and touch a whole new generation of criminals who had never heard his name.

Unfortunately for Thaddeus, the yellow pages saw her coming. They had brochures and full-color graphs and charts and columns of figures, all proving how lawyers *in exactly Thaddeus's situation* could quadruple their business by putting their own, personal message right there in yellow and black in front of every criminal in the greater dialing area.

The fact that the particular full-page message they had in mind cost $40,000 a year—well, with easy monthly payments, Thaddeus could guarantee himself financial security. Busloads of criminals, they told Jolene, would be showing up at his door just as soon as he signed on their dotted line. So, he signed and went to work supporting the phone company.

All he needed to make his ad a reality was an 8½-by-11, black-and-white glossy of himself, and a slogan. The picture was easy enough. He arranged his face into a street-smart-yet-compassionate look that conveyed his steely determination to protect the criminal element from the machinations of a hopelessly corrupt justice system, and the photographer snapped away.

The slogan was even easier. Thaddeus knew what people wanted in a lawyer. His own clients had told him often enough, once they discovered what they had actually gotten. And, he came up with a slogan announcing to the criminal community that their long search was over: *At last! An honest lawyer.*

By the time the yellow pages came out, Thaddeus's ad had been reviewed by his director of marketing and tweaked and adjusted in accordance with the most current theories of human psychology, every one of which Jolene had read books about. Thaddeus, himself, reviewed the final version with the same care and attention he lavished on all his professional matters, so it wasn't until six months later when the yellow pages finally hit the streets that he discovered what his $40,000 had actually bought. The straightforward, if somewhat misleading, sentiment about finding an honest lawyer had transmogrified into the much more ambiguous

Alas, an honest lawyer!

By then tax season had come and gone, and Jolene had achieved immortal status at Thaddeus Silk & Assoc.—which is why she was still on the payroll three years later.

I liked Jolene. She was a quiet girl, and appealing, she always seemed so lost and eager to please. She was tall, and shapely. She had red hair, and she slouched a bit, as if she were embarrassed to call any more attention to her breasts than they called to themselves. Her clothes were much cheaper and more rumpled than would have been considered good form at most law firms. But, then, most law firms wouldn't have let her keep beer at her desk.

She was also an Indian. "Pure, one-eighth Nehalem, at least her mother is. Comes from down by Depoe Bay," Thaddeus told me. "Her dad worked on a road crew." Thaddeus had hired her through some kind of work-release program under which the state paid him to rehabilitate criminals.

By the time I showed up, he had disbanded his marketing department—which is to say, he had moved Jolene to the desk in the reception area. Sometimes she would answer the phone, then jot down a message on a pink piece of paper in case Thaddeus ever cared to check on who'd called. Mostly, though, she read books on history and biography and science and whatever other high-class reading matter she could lay her hands on.

The morning Thaddeus died, the police were still in the office collecting evidence from his credenza when the phone rang. Jolene, always on the alert, answered politely, then covered the mouthpiece and whispered something to Sophie.

"That *slut*," Sophie bellowed across the room and out the door and over the city at large, "is Thaddeus's girlfriend."

That *slut* turned out to be Abby Birdsong, and Sophie was wrong about the girlfriend part. At least, Abby wasn't the girlfriend Thaddeus had been with the night he'd had his first heart attack. Abby was just somebody who'd once worked in a bar Thaddeus had owned a long time ago.

Even if Sophie had been right, having Abby Birdsong as a girlfriend wasn't any great accomplishment. As far as I made out later, Abby had been girlfriend to every single adult male, and a couple of unadult males, as well, who had ventured anywhere near the Oregon Coast in the early seventies. Of course, I didn't know any of that the day she called. All I knew then was that she sounded slender and elegant with a vaguely New England accent. And she needed a lawyer. She had been busted at Rooster Rock State Park with a little over an ounce of marijuana in her purse.

As sexy as her voice sounded, the idea that she had been at Rooster Rock was even sexier. Rooster Rock State Park is a nude beach on the Columbia River and is just the place to attract the free-and-easy sort of spirits who might want to blow a few jays. It's also the kind of place that attracts the attention of county deputies wanting to keep an eye on what's going on.

All this was a quarter century ago. I was younger then, and not pushing the wrong side of middle age. Some say I was better looking, too. I was certainly more impressed by nudity than I am now—especially when slender ladies with New England accents were involved. Besides, with Thaddeus out of the picture and no prospects of anybody else signing my next paycheck, building up a client base of my own seemed like a good idea. And what better place to start building than with Thaddeus's client list? Nobody, I calculated, needed a lawyer more than one of Thaddeus's clients. So I took Abby's case right there on the phone, without knowing anything else about her. Just the picture of someone slender with her elegant voice swimming naked at Rooster Rock was enough to start us off on a solid, professional relationship. We made an appointment for her to come by at two the next afternoon.

4

TWO O'CLOCK CAME and went with no sign of Abby Birdsong, and I was feeling let down about it. I wanted to get a look at the woman with the cool, seductive voice who spent her time naked at Rooster Rock.

Even without the nude swimming, Rooster Rock is an automatically sexy place. It is an enormous basalt formation that stands in the full pride of its manhood on the narrow strip of land between Interstate 84 and the Columbia River. And *manhood* is not a false cognate. Rooster Rock may be the largest—it is certainly the most explicit—natural rendition of an erect penis anywhere on the planet. Why anybody would name it after a chicken was beyond me.

Abby, on the other hand, is a pretty name. As New England as her voice. But Birdsong? What kind of name is Birdsong?

Maybe she wasn't New England at all, I told myself. Maybe she was the half-white child of another culture—a culture that revered all things living and smoked sacred plants to honor Nature and the Oneness of All. Maybe that's what she had been doing at Rooster Rock when she was busted. Maybe I was about to get the opportunity to argue a religious-rights case all the way to the United States Supreme Court.

Maybe she would show up.

Instead, the police came. They still had a few questions, and as the last surviving member of the firm of Thaddeus Silk & Assoc., I was elected to come up with the answers.

"What time did you roll into work yesterday?" a beefy policeman asked as he led me into Thaddeus's office.

"About nine forty-five," I told him. The same blond policewoman who had been trying to keep the news crews from trampling evidence closed the door behind us.

"We got you down for ten twenty." The beefy policeman gestured for me to sit in a chair pulled out into the middle of the office. "That sound more like it?"

"Ten twenty." I thought back over when I had come in. That could be. "Things were confusing."

"Right." The beefy policeman shoved a stack of files onto the floor, then sat in Thaddeus's chair. "You usually come waltzing in at ten-twenty?"

"Sometimes."

"Mostly you show up about eight thirty." The way he said it, it wasn't a question.

I nodded. This guy knew more about my habits than made me comfortable.

The blond policewoman shoved aside another stack of files and perched on the couch at the back of the office where I couldn't see her, making me feel even more uncomfortable.

The beefy cop slid Thaddeus's phone to the side of the desk, knocking more papers to the floor. Then he reached for the answering machine. Only it wasn't an answering machine. It was a tape recorder hooked to the phone.

"I bet this thing doesn't give those little beeps to let the other party know he's being recorded." Beefy Cop smiled past me to the blond policewoman in the back of the office. He had coarse, black hair and a rough face that made me wonder whether he had once been a prize-fighter. And he had a vein throbbing over his left temple that made me worry about his health. All in all, he was a very convincing bad cop.

"Doubt it," the blond policewoman said from somewhere behind my chair.

"I doubt it, too." Beefy Cop laid the tape recorder on top of a pile of papers with a look of distaste. Then he turned toward me, making me feel like a criminal just for working for Thaddeus. "Why were you so late?"

"I was up late." It was as good a reason as any.

"You were up late because you were here the night Mr. Silk died." That didn't seem like a question, either.

"*No.*" I must have sounded a little rattled. "I was home."

"Home?" He wrote something on his notepad to use against me later. Then he glared at me as if he were still a prizefighter. "Where did that money in the safe come from?"

"Search me," I said, and a little too late realized that "search me" might not be the perfect answer to give an angry policeman who was on the hunt for evidence.

"You were Thaddeus Silk's partner and you're trying to tell me you don't know where the money in his safe came from?" He stared in disbelief.

I shook my head, feeling as if I should know.

"That gold that Ms. Silk . . ." He waved in disgust in the general direction of Sophie's desk out front. "You know anything about that missing treasure of hers?"

I shook my head, again. And then, waited while he struggled to gain control over his emotions.

"You are sitting there telling me you don't know what Thaddeus Silk, *your* partner—" Another pile of papers slid off the desk and hit the floor.

"*Associate,*" I interrupted. Being Thaddeus Silk's partner was an honor I wanted no part of. Partners, they told us in law school, are responsible for each other's actions. "I was his associate."

"Associate. Partner. Whatever." The vein in his forehead was throbbing so violently I wondered whether he was about to become the second person to drop dead in Thaddeus's office.

"You mean to sit there and tell me . . . tell *her*"—Blond Policewoman was wading around to the front of the office so she could aim her most disappointed look at me—"that you don't have the slightest idea what Mr. Silk . . ." Beefy Cop gave up and slumped back in Thaddeus's chair as if the depth of my stupidity had defeated him.

21

After a while, he stood and kicked his way through piles of paper until he was looming over my chair, making me feel claustrophobic. *"Look,"* he told me. "I'm going to the can. When I get back, I expect you to be more . . ." He trailed off, figuring I already knew what he expected me to be more of.

When he was gone, Ms. Blond Policewoman came over and put her hand on my shoulder. "I can handle Rocco," she said. "But you've got to help me out here. Just tell him what he wants and he'll file his report and you won't ever hear from us again. This is a big deal for him."

I nodded, starting to feel that whatever Thaddeus had been up to, I was in it as deep as he'd been. And the only thing for me to do was to fess up, cop a plea, turn state's evidence, and come clean over the whole sordid matter.

She gave my shoulder a little squeeze. "You're not the one we're after." I was flooded with gratitude. For a good cop, she was pretty convincing, as well.

Funny how that worked. I knew they were playing it for my benefit. For all I could tell, in real life she was a brass-plated bitch and Rocco spent his weekends delivering baskets of gumdrops to orphans. But knowing they were playing good-cop-bad-cop didn't make me feel any better. Right then, what I wanted was for the blond policewoman to like me, and for Rocco not to be mad at me.

It wasn't until I went to bed that night that a couple of things crossed my mind. The first was "Rocco"? That thug's name was "Rocco"? They'd been laying it on pretty thick.

The other was "This is a big deal for him." That penny-ante investigation Sophie had kicked into gear with her talk about missing Spanish treasure and late-night intruders and murder-by-surprise wouldn't be a big deal for anybody. Whatever those two were after, they had been after it long before Sophie ever dialed 911.

When Beefy Cop came back from the bathroom, he almost sounded civil. He went over the same ground a couple more times just in case Ms. Good Cop's squeeze on my shoulder had jogged my memory.

Then, he leaned toward me in a way that made me think he was about to ask the most important question of the interview and wanted to know, Who is Engine Joe?

Engine Joe? I didn't have a clue.

"*Who* is Engine Joe?" he tried again.

I thought about making a joke about the mechanic who worked on Thaddeus's beat-up old Dodge, but it didn't seem like a good plan, and I shook my head. By then, I was starting to hope they'd ask something I could answer. But *Engine Joe?*

"Take your time," Blond Policewoman said from over my shoulder. "Just tell us what you know."

"Nothing." I shook my head, again. "I never heard of any—"

"This yardbird wants us to believe"—Rocco wrote carefully onto his notepad as if he were a court reporter taking down sworn testimony—"that Thaddeus Silk, his partner—"

"Associate. I was his associate."

"—never mentioned Engine Joe the whole time they worked together . . ." He stopped writing and glared a glare that would have scared everything I knew about Engine Joe out of me, if I had known anything about Engine Joe.

". . . or any little . . . sideline . . . businesses he and Mr. Silk might have been running out of this office. Is *that* it?" From the way he phrased it, I couldn't tell whether the *he* Thaddeus had been running the sideline business with was Engine Joe or me.

"That's about the size of it," I told him back. That bad-cop act of his was beginning to wear thin.

"And," he said as they stood to leave, "he wants us to believe he wasn't here the night Mr. Silk died."

"You can write that down, too," I told him as the blond policewoman shot me a disappointed look. Then they disappeared through the door and were gone, and I wondered how much they really knew about where I had been the night Thaddeus died.

5

FOR A WHILE, Sophie parked herself at her usual post in the waiting
area, bellowing secrets and client confidences and glittering bits of
insanity into the air like badly choreographed fireworks. I'm not sure
why she still came in. Sometimes I think she just wanted to hold on
to her brother a little longer.

She spent a lot of time on the phone yelling at the police about
the treasure missing from Thaddeus's safe. "It's *mine* and it's worth
millions and I want it back." I was beginning to develop a lot of
sympathy for our brothers in blue. "I'll have my law firm come down
and . . . *What . . . is . . . your . . . name?* . . . Because I can tell you one
thing, *Officer* Randolph, the first name on the indictment is going to
be Theodore H. Randolph the Third, and by the time Thaddeus Silk
and Associates is finished with you, you won't even be sweeping the
streets in this . . ."

Whatever else was going to happen to Officer Theodore H. Randolph
III, he never found out. Before Sophie could tell him, she got so mad
she slammed down the receiver and hung up on herself.

One morning she yelled into the phone in a tone that implied the
strictest confidence that Thaddie had been keeping the treasure to sell
for a private investor. Then she must have suspected she had said too
much and glanced around the reception area to make sure none of us
had heard.

After a few seconds, she went back to her private, for-your-ears-
only bellow and described what sounded very much like a fencing
operation with the late Thaddeus Silk, Esq., at the center. "He had
bracelets and rings made out of pure gold, and other rings set with

rubies, and a four-hundred-year-old, solid-gold crucifix like Spanish aristocrats wear, or the pope, and he had a gold brooch with a huge emerald. And now it's all stolen and nobody can find any of it, and what am I going to *do*?" Suddenly, I understood who had ransacked Thaddeus's office the morning Sophie had found him dead.

Jolene spent her days at the reception desk reading and, every now and then, answering the phone. It was hard to see why Thaddeus Silk & Assoc. still needed a receptionist, since all we were doing was closing up the firm, but I was going to keep Jolene around as long as I could. I liked her and I was worried about where she would go once the office shut down. Back to jail, I supposed.

If Jolene was a diamond in the rough, her boyfriend was the curse that came with it. Tail Pipe was big, with the filthy, disheveled look of the professional Vietnam veteran during the eighties. But, with Tail Pipe it wasn't a fashion statement.

He spent his days lounging in the reception area staring at the wall and sneaking looks at Jolene. Sometimes, when he didn't think anyone else was around, he would talk to her in a gentle, cracked baritone. I couldn't ever hear what he said, but it made her smile and look up at him—the one love of her hard, strung-out life.

I never discovered what had happened to Tail Pipe in Vietnam. Something to do with rockets and a squad of North Vietnamese regulars. Or, maybe, it was fragmentation grenades and a clumsy supply sergeant. Or, perhaps, an overwrought tank of CO_2 gas at the enlisted men's club. The story drifted a little every time he told it. But, whatever it was, it had been bad. Uncle only gives you 40 percent disability if your entire arm is blown off, and Tail Pipe was a double-dipper in the disabled-veteran department—signed on for a full 100 percent on account of what had happened to his body. And signed on all over again for a second full 100 percent for what had become of the rest of him. Which meant that Tail Pipe earned more wallowing semiconscious in the waiting area than any of the rest of us took home from working sixty- and seventy-hour weeks. It was almost as if Tail Pipe had won the lottery for unlucky people. Still, it was hard to resent him. Anybody with a 100 percent disability earns his check every day.

Sitting in the waiting area, sneaking glances at Jolene and listening to Sophie bellow into the phone, gave him time to think. And, sometimes, he would come up with questions I wish I had asked. Like, Why do they call you jarheads?

When he asked that, Sophie, former marine, ex-jarhead that she was, hung up on whomever she was haranguing and turned her full attention to Tail Pipe. To the person on the other end, it must have seemed like a miracle.

Here I am, you could almost hear her thinking, *a member of the United States Marine Corps and this . . . this INFANTRYman . . . this DOG . . . FACED . . . infantryman . . .* She gave up at the effrontery of it all and slumped in her swivel chair. It was the only time I ever saw Sophie defeated.

But she had grit. She shook her head, forgot about Tail Pipe, picked up the phone, and began dialing the number of her next victim.

It didn't seem to bother Tail Pipe that Sophie ignored his question. Most people ignored him. Besides, all he really wanted was to be near Jolene. He loved her with a deep and abiding love you don't often see, and it touches your heart when you do. Glancing at Jolene and thinking about Jolene and being near Jolene were the chief pleasures in Tail Pipe's life. That, and beer.

I spent most of my time those first few days going through the mess in Thaddeus's office, trying to figure out what I needed to tell his clients. There turned out to be a lot less there than met the eye, though. Almost all of the files had been closed long ago. Still, it was going to take weeks to make sure I hadn't missed something.

6

A WEEK OR so after Abby Birdsong didn't show up, Grady Jackson called, and I had my first real client. My first task was to drive down to Eugene and interview the archaeologist who had been working for him when he was thrown off the beach. She turned out to be talkative.

"It's been ten years, and you know how many times I've had to testify about what happened that afternoon? *Five* times." She grimaced. "Once for the hearing and four more times in those lawsuits he keeps filing. And, now, here *you* are, starting it up all over again."

I nodded. It was pretty clear from the rattle of words she wasn't expecting conversation.

"I don't know what I could have been thinking." She shrugged the shrug of the misunderstood. "There isn't any archaeology *in* Oregon. People think it's all Nazis and secret passages and hidden tombs"—*Raiders of the Lost Ark* had just come out and she had a picture of herself on her desk looking dashing in a leather jacket and broad-brimmed felt hat—"but it's nothing like that." She gestured around the small office. "Mostly, it's just paperwork."

She was right about the paperwork. Boxes of paper were everywhere.

"You wouldn't think a state that didn't have any archaeology would require so much paper about archaeology. But that's what it's come to. The archaeology of the paper midden . . ." She was a slender woman with a mobile face, jeans, and a cable-knit sweater that fit well with her position on the faculty of the University of Oregon.

"I dig through layers of paper for traces of anything I can use. And, let me tell you something. There's damn little in there. Half this stuff is about Grady Jackson, and I didn't stay with for him for more than a couple of months." She began rummaging through a box. "*Here* it is . . . I got it on paper, so it's real."

She pulled out a report and handed it to me. "If he's so eager to get back on the beach, why did he close down that afternoon? Weather was good, and you don't get much of that on the Oregon Coast in October, and the tide was going out, and he just shut down and sent me home."

The report was dated Tuesday, 19 October 1971—Grady's last day on Neahkahnie Beach.

"My first job out of archaeology school and all I get to do is watch Grady Jackson pull junk out of the sand and tell everybody he's on the trail of the lost treasure of the Incas. The state made him hire somebody to keep an eye on what he dug up, and I thought it would be fun. If I'd had a halfway decent Spanish teacher, I'd be down in Peru, studying *real* Inca treasure. But not with Señorita Sigridsdottir. No chance of that."

She paused for breath, then launched in, again. "Most of these flakes go broke and disappear. But not Grady. Grady Jackson just keeps throwing money at these lawsuits . . . Anybody ever tell you about what happened when they tried to get him to make his bed in the army?"

I nodded, again.

"Well, he's like that about this treasure hunt. If I hadn't been there and seen for myself, I might think he really had found something. But it couldn't have been much, just a strange rock or an old bit of pipe." She shook her head in consternation.

"That's why he sent me home, so he could come back and dig without me watching. The next day, the neighbors complained about him running his backhoe at night and the state kicked him off the beach. That's when I went from being a professional archaeologist to being a professional archaeology witness. I could have gone into ethnography." She spread her hands in a but-what-can-you-do kind of way.

"I like people. I would have been a good ethnographer. In archaeology, any schizo who pulls a rusty skillet out of the sand can claim it's a sign because Pachacuti Inca Yupanqui always buried one of his mirrors to let you know when you were on the right track. In ethnography, you try a thing like that and an informant is going to march straight to a professor from another university and explain how it's a skillet, and you're going to have egg all over your face. Not that Grady stayed on the trail of Inca treasure for long. After he started digging, he found out about Sir Francis Drake, and all of a sudden we were looking for the Lost Colony of New Albion. That's the way it is with these psychos. I should write a paper."

She jotted a note to herself, as if it were the first time the idea of writing a paper had occurred to her. "They go from looking for objects out of the Bible, to Inca gold, to Sir Francis Drake's treasure, and back again, and it all seems perfectly normal to them. My dad had been on Guadalcanal. Grady was a kind of a legend around our house and this was my first job, so I was rooting for him to hit it big. But all I ever saw were bits of iron and old hinges and car parts. If Señorita Sigridsdottir had been any good, I'd be doing real archaeology now, instead of talking to lawyers all the time."

"Señorita Sigridsdottir," I interrupted. "You had a Spanish teacher named Señorita Sigridsdottir?"

"That was one more thing I was never quite sure about," she said, as if she'd collected decades of things she wasn't quite sure about. "If she'd been a real Bolivian princess like she always claimed, instead of some kind of minority hire the administration tossed at us because filling their quotas was more important than whether we learned Spanish, I'd be in Peru now. But I wouldn't have qualified." She sighed at the unfairness of it all. "Those Latin America jobs all went to affirmative-action babies."

"You mean"—that was a new one on me—"there's some kind of minority-hiring program in archaeology?"

"Who else do you think"—she looked at me as if I were naïve—"grows up speaking Spanish at home?"

7

THE ODD PART about Grady's treasure hunt was that there might have been something to it, at least if you believed the stories circulating around the Oregon Coast when the settlers started arriving.

In 1848, the Tillamooks told a settler named John Hobson as good a version as any: Long ago, a ship like a huge bird anchored off Neahkahnie Beach. Strange, pale men aided by a black demon lugged a box up the mountain and buried it, but before they filled the hole, the pale men murdered the demon and tossed his body on top of the box. The box is supposed to be there still. With the ghost of a black demon on guard, the Indians left the place alone. A detail that turned out to be important when farmers started plowing up strangely marked rocks at the foot of Neahkahnie Mountain is that, before leaving, the sailors stuck around long enough to chisel markings into rocks.

That's the basic story, and it's easy to convince yourself there's something to it. But how much of that something is true is impossible to say. Long before there were settlers to write them down, the stories had budded and branched and divided into so many different versions, nobody alive knew what had really happened. We don't know that much. Whatever those long-ago Indians remembered, we can only see through the eyes of the early whites—who embellished and embroidered what they heard with the hopes and half-truths of a whole new race of storytellers, until all we have are legends of legends—white-man stories about Indian stories. But there are a lot of them.

Sometimes, it's not a black shipmate who's murdered, it's witnesses. Or the black man has changed into a whole party of sailors, and the murder into an argument that gets ugly. Other tales aren't of treasure, but of shipwreck. A Nehalem named Mrs. Gervais told how a group of her people had been making their way along the beach when they came across mounds of strange objects and the remains of a monstrous canoe. Working in the wreckage were thirty oddly dressed white men who told them through signs that they had come across the water and run aground during the night.

In another legend, it's not one ship, it's three fighting offshore. Watching from Neahkahnie Mountain, the Indians could see the ships throwing smoke at each other until two sank. Then the third ran itself onto the beach for repairs. When the repairs were finished, the sailors tried to push her back into the water but lost control, and she broke up in the surf, strewing equipment all over the beach.

Some stories even claim to be based on eyewitness accounts. In 1852, Thomas Vaughn met an old woman who told him that, when she was a girl, she had actually seen the treasure buried. Her story is as well documented as any white-man legend because Vaughn wrote it down in his diary. The woman told him she and her mother had been picking berries on Neahkahnie Mountain when the men came ashore and buried the box. She even showed him where it was buried, but said that, years before, the mountain had slid down, so it was a long way underground by then. Based on his estimate of how old the woman was, Vaughn calculated the box must have been buried some-time in the 1780s.

The Tillamooks told a story that's easy to dismiss as a fantasy—until you hear the odd, modern sequel: Sailors dragged their ship onto Three Rocks Beach a few miles south of Neahkahnie, to repair the hull. At first, they got along with the Indians. They swapped blankets and tools for fresh meat and water, and everybody would have parted friends if the sailors had been any good at carpentry. They weren't, though. When they relaunched the ship, it sank—but not until the sailors had rowed ashore with a large chest filled with gold coins and jewels.

Unfortunately, they chose to hide it in a burial ground and, when the Tillamooks complained, ran them off with swords and guns. A few days later, most of the sailors headed inland to look for other white men, but a couple stayed behind to guard the spot where the treasure was buried.

One was skinny with a long, drooping mustache. The other was a huge black man, seven feet tall with enormous muscles. The black man must have been mute because, during the week they were there, he never said a word. The skinny guy never shut up. He danced around with a sword pretending to attack his companion. Sometimes he cut him and drew trickles of blood. Finally, the black man couldn't stand it anymore and broke his head.

With the white guy out of the picture, the Tillamooks asked the black man to leave. He refused. A warrior hurled a lance. The black man broke it over his knee, then broke the neck of the nearest Indian, only to find himself filled with arrows. The warriors kicked and beat him to death with clubs, then buried him beside the white guy, and that was that. At least until the 1930s.

Black men are specifically mentioned in so many stories, and described in such detail, it's impossible to believe the Indians never actually met any. Whoever these black men were, and however many the Indians saw, they may not have all been killed. Some may have married into the tribes. Kilchis, a chief of the Tillamooks, lived until at least 1862, giving plenty of settlers the chance to comment on his dark skin, kinky hair, flat nose, high forehead, and long chin.

In the 1860s, a settler named Daniel L. Pike met a black man who claimed to be the only survivor of a group of sailors who had been murdered by the Indians when their treasure ship had wrecked at the foot of Neahkahnie Mountain. According to the black man, the crew waded ashore, buried their treasure, then moved in with the Nehalems. The black man hammered a knife out of a bit of iron and gave it to the chief. The knife may have saved his life because, when the Nehalems killed the rest of the crew, they made a slave of him instead. Later, when the chief took him along to Astoria, he escaped and made his way to the Coast Range, where he met Dan Pike.

Word got around, and a group of settlers tried to talk the black man into leading them to the treasure. He refused to go anywhere near Neahkahnie Mountain because he thought the chief was still looking for him. Eventually, he went as far as Astoria, where he died of smallpox. But, not before drawing a map. The map was accurate enough to prove he had been to Neahkahnie, but not enough to lead to the treasure.

People with white ancestors were living among the Indians, too. In 1811, Gabriel Franchere, one of John Jacob Astor's fur traders, met an old man named Soto who said his father was one of four Spaniards who had been shipwrecked on the Clatsop's beach. He had tried to walk back to civilization, but he didn't make it any farther than the Cascade Mountains, where he married Soto's mother.

Astor's men also met a half-white Clatsop named Lamazee, who told them his father had been shipwrecked in the 1760s. Lamazee had more than just pale skin to back up his story. He had a tattoo with the name Jack Ramsey.

Lewis and Clark met yet another man whose ancestors may have traced back to a wreck. He was a Clatsop named Cullaby. Cullaby had freckles and long, dusky red hair. He was about twenty-five years old and was at least half-white. He told Lewis and Clark that, in about 1760, his ancestor had been shipwrecked and married into the tribe.

If Cullaby knew what he was talking about, then sailors must have been washing up on Oregon beaches for years because a redhead could not have been the son of a pure Indian and a sailor. Red hair is governed by a recessive gene so, no matter how red a sailor's head, his children would all have had the black hair of their mother. Which means Cullaby's mother must already have carried the redhead gene—making her the partially white descendant of an even earlier sailor.

In one legend, the wrecked ship was Chinese. A crewman waded ashore, built a new ship, turned pirate, and began raiding up and down the coast. As with all these stories, there are just enough supporting facts to make one wonder. Seventeenth-century Chinese coins sometimes show up in Indian burial sites, as do arrowheads made out of broken bits of Ming porcelain. And, if that isn't enough, something like seventy-five medieval junks have positively been identified along the coast of North America.

One of the oddest stories dates from 1931. E. G. Calkins decided to build a commercial campground at Three Rocks Beach and, when he leveled the area, dug up human bones. Lots of them.

Calkins took the bones to Dr. F. M. Carter, a physician who studied Northwest Indians, and to Dr. John Horner, a specialist in Oregon history. One skeleton was from a man more than seven feet tall. The rest were much smaller. Dr. Carter determined the smaller skeletons belonged to Indians and were probably taken from a burial ground. The larger skeleton was from a black man. The way his bones had been broken suggested he had been tortured or beaten to death.

The story of the bones hit the papers, rumors about treasure reached Calkins, and he beat feet back to his campground. He dug some holes, but he couldn't tell where the skeletons had been. After a while, he gave up and went back to renting campsites.

8

TWENTY-THREE DAYS AFTER Abby Birdsong bagged our meeting, I was on the phone, trying to explain to a gentleman from the Oregon State Bar that I didn't really know anything about how Thaddeus handled his trust accounts, when she showed up, operating on Marijuana Standard Time. One look at her, and my fantasies of swimming naked in the Columbia splashed around my ankles.

Abby was fair-skinned, although *fair* is an exaggeration. *Mealy* was more like it, as if she didn't get out much. Her face was round with double chins, almost invisible eyebrows, and what looked like acne under the dull light of the waiting area. Taken all in all, it was not a sexy face.

On the plus side, her posture was good. But, then, it's skinny people who have the luxury to slouch. When you are carrying as much weight as Abby hauled around, try to slouch and you get a crick in your back. And she had wonderful thick, dark hair.

It hung in a braid as big around as my wrist, and almost to her knees. It was set off with a pair of tortoise-shell combs, and it shone, as if she spent hours brushing it. For someone otherwise so careless of her looks, Abby took pride in that hair. She must have gotten a lot of compliments on it when she was younger and men paid more attention to her. At a guess, I would have said she was forty-five.

As much as anybody I ever met, Abby Birdsong was truly a Bride of the Weed. The afternoon she finally made it to my office, and every time I met with her from then on, she stank of marijuana as if she stored her clothes in a smokehouse of dope. And she didn't just smell of dope, she carried a large straw bag that dribbled seeds as she walked.

I had no way of checking, but I'm almost certain she kept a couple of pounds in there. The more I talked to her over the months, the harder it was to pin down exactly what else she did with her life other than toke up.

And, then, she toked up right in my office.

I've smelled some bad dope in my time, but whatever it was Abby was dribbling out of her straw bag gave new meaning to the word *shit*. That was, hands down, the worst dope I ever smelled.

It was difficult to imagine, but she hadn't started life as a dope-head. Years earlier she had been, of all things, a logger. And, from the people I talked to, a real feminist tiger, at that—a regular shock trooper of the women's revolution until the day a choker cable snapped when she was in range. After she got out of the hospital, she waited tables at the bar Thaddeus used to own over on the Coast. That lasted until she drifted away into her own world with a jay hanging from her mouth. Since then, she'd been doing nothing in particular. Nothing in particular, that is, unless you count smoking dope as something. In which case, she had been very busy.

The part I couldn't figure was how she could afford to buy all that dope. Maybe, it crossed my mind more than once, the deputy who'd arrested her at Rooster Rock was right. Maybe she really did sell the stuff. And, in Oregon, the difference between selling and using is a big difference, indeed.

The marijuana laws here aren't like they are where you live. Here, owning marijuana isn't a crime—at least if you are caught with less than an ounce, in which case the police write what amounts to a traffic ticket, and you go home and fire up a doobie at the indignity of it all. Get caught with more than an ounce, and you're looking at possession for sales, and some serious cell time.

Unfortunately for Abby, the little over an ounce the deputy found in her purse turned out to weigh 2.31 pounds. If I couldn't get that fact thrown out, I was going to have to convince a jury that carrying almost two and a third pounds of marijuana to a place famous around the state as an outdoor drug bazaar didn't necessarily mean Abby was a drug dealer. In Abby's case, it just meant she smoked a lot of dope. A whole lot of dope.

"That traffic stop was *bull*shit," Abby told me, then took a long toke to soothe her nerves. "Here I was driving through Rooster Rock minding my own business when this construction worker jumps out and waves a stop-sign-on-a-stick in front of my car like he thinks I'm supposed to stop." Abby's voice began to turn shrill, she was so upset at the unfairness of it all. "Well, I'd just been retested for my driver's license, and I had the *Oregon Driver Manual* right there in the car." She shoved a copy at me to use as evidence. "And it doesn't say thing *one* about construction workers directing traffic."

I could only imagine what Abby had done to cause herself to have to be retested for her driver's license.

"I mean, if they were so worried about their precious asphalt, they should have put a cop out there to keep people from running through it."

I nodded at her to keep going.

"The next thing I know, I'm being run off the road by this huge asphalt truck and then up comes Deputy A. W. Bolt and he makes all four of us get out, and before we can tell him about those construction workers, he's got his hands down my purse and *I'm* the one who's busted. Here I am, run off the road by a gang of construction workers impersonating the law, and then the *real* law comes up and he busts *me*." Abby sputtered to a stop, looking for me to weave a defense out of these unjust facts.

Only, I couldn't see it. If anything, that construction-worker story was just going to convince the jury that Abby had been too doped up to be behind the wheel of a car.

"All that deputy did"—she blew out a cloud of smoke in disgust—"was catch me with more than an ounce of shit. That and a movie camera. But there's no law against having a movie camera in your car. We never took it anywhere but in the men's room, so it wasn't like we were trying to make movies of naked people out on the beach, or anything. We were just—"

Whoa, I thought. *You didn't say anything about movie cameras when you called.* "You were in the men's room at Rooster Rock State Park with a movie camera?"

"They got this sign on the door and—"

"You . . . were taking . . . *movies*," I said slowly, hoping the implications might sink in, "in . . . the . . . men's . . . *bath*room?"

Abby seemed perplexed that I would even raise the issue. "That was the whole point of *being* at Rooster Rock. If they're going to put those public bathrooms out there with those signs like that, then they've got to expect members of the public will—"

"There were *men* in the bathroom?"

"Just a couple of guys at the urinals."

"And they were . . . ?"

"Of *course* they were. Why *else* would anybody stand in front of a urinal?"

"And did you . . . *ask* . . . those . . . men . . . for . . . *permission* . . . to . . . film?"

"If we asked *permission*"—Abby looked at me as if she were wondering what kind of lawyer she had hired—"what would have been the point of taking the movies?"

I let it drop. The district attorney hadn't charged her with taking movies in the men's room, and until he did, it was the dope I had to worry about. Until then, that camera was just one more piece of prejudicial evidence I was going to have to keep the jury from finding out about.

There was one other thing about Abby. While she was sitting in my office, I got a good look at her face. Another woman might have dabbed on a little makeup, but Abby Birdsong was never much for covering the truth. Frankly, I'm not sure she had ever used makeup in her life. As a feminist firebrand, she would never have objectified herself that way. Then, as a round-the-clock doper, she wouldn't have cared. Which meant, even in the dim light in my office, I could see the scar running across her forehead, and over her eye, and onto her cheek.

9

NOT LONG AFTER I met with Abby Birdsong, I discovered that Thaddeus might have had a reason to keep his office a pigsty. Those files scattered around the floor were the perfect place to hide documents.

A couple of Koreans were in the waiting room that morning. At least, I think they were Koreans. They certainly looked Korean. They were handsome people, neatly dressed and dignified. They were also late middle-aged and modest, a man and a woman, and polite in the manner of people who feel out of place.

Jolene said they were waiting for Sophie. If they were, they were in for a long wait. Sophie hadn't been seen in the office for two weeks, not since the afternoon she'd figured out the police weren't going to bring the stolen treasure back.

Tail Pipe was shifting around in his usual chair, dark and shaggy and smelling like month-old beer. The Koreans were across from him, knees almost touching his in the tiny space. From time to time they smiled polite smiles and nodded little half-bows in his direction.

His head wobbled in semiconscious reply, the wobbles of an early-morning drunk trying to adjust to the unexpected presence of strangers materialized in his midst. But, he wouldn't have been Tail Pipe if he didn't try to rise to the occasion. "I . . . don't . . ." He hesitated, searching for the perfect icebreaker to make strangers feel at home. "I . . . I don't have any . . . belly button . . ."

He looked at the two startled people for a moment, groping for the perfect words to establish his we-are-all-in-this-together brotherhood-ness with them. ". . . *either*!" He grinned. "I don't have any belly button, either."

The Koreans smiled back and nodded and bowed shallow bows, as if he were right, as if they, too, did not have belly buttons. I could have told them it was a mistake.

Encouraged, Tail Pipe pulled up his shirt to show exactly where he didn't have a belly button. "See," he said as if not having a belly button was the greatest accomplishment of his life. "*No* belly button."

He was right about the no-belly-button part. His whole abdomen was a mass of scars.

"I was lying on my back," he told them seriously, "when Charlie shot my ass off."

A few seconds earlier, Tail Pipe had been the one who hadn't known what to say. Now it was the Koreans who were at a loss. They smiled and half-bowed, again, but their hearts weren't in it. They glanced at each other, stood, gave a couple of additional half-bows. And were out of there—leaving Tail Pipe to slump back in his self-induced catatonia and stare at the wall. If it hadn't been for the little glimpses in Jolene's direction, you would have thought he was unconscious.

That was the morning I found the file nobody but Thaddeus was supposed to see. It was the one he had been working on the night he died. I recognized it from the bourbon rings, and as soon as I did, I knew I had to look inside. At the very least, I was going to have to call the client and explain about needing a new lawyer. But when I picked up the file, it concerned a matter that had closed twenty-three years earlier. And, strangest of all, the words *Working Documents* were written across the tab—which meant the file was the final earthly resting place of the unfinished pleadings, half-done memos, drafts of letters that were never sent, notes about strategy, and all the other dead ends and false starts that should have been thrown away twenty-three years before when the case closed. I couldn't imagine why Thaddeus would have had such a file open on his desk.

Inside was pretty much what you would expect to find in a twenty-three-year-old working-documents file, at least at first glance. An unexecuted second mortgage on a piece of land in Cannon Beach, along with half a dozen drafts of letters from January and February of 1958. And,

44

then, I found the reason. Tucked behind the mortgage was an accounting sheet. And, written across the top of the sheet, in Thaddeus's handwriting, was *Engine Joe*. Whoever Engine Joe was, it was a sure bet nobody else in the world ever called him that. That name was Thaddeus's last line of defense in case the file landed in the wrong hands.

A neat column of abbreviations ran down the side of the sheet:

Rng
Brclt
Slvr Ptchr

Ring. Bracelet. Silver Pitcher, if I didn't miss my guess. And a lot more. Silver Drinking Cup. Gold Crucifix. And coins and tableware and on and on.

There was one item I didn't have to guess at, though.

Sm Gld Brch w/Em

Small Gold Brooch with Emerald. I had seen it myself, in Thaddeus's safe the night he died.

The abbreviations were followed by cash entries in all sorts of amounts from just a few dollars to well over $10,000 for a pair of gold candlesticks. It was exactly what I would have expected the records of a fencing operation to look like. No wonder the police wanted to know about Engine Joe.

The last few entries were dated the night Thaddeus died, so I'm pretty sure it was the sheet he'd been working on when I'd come into his office. The cash amounts weren't filled in, though, as if he'd logged in the items, but hadn't lived long enough to dispose of them. I was still staring at those entries when Jolene announced I had a phone call.

It was the blond policewoman, and she couldn't have been a gooder cop. She hated to bother me. She apologized for even calling. She just wanted to know when it would be convenient for me to drop by for a lie-detector test.

10

THREE DAYS LATER, I was in the offices of Lydia Stonemason. After the call about the lie-detector test, I figured I needed a lawyer of my own, and Lydia was the best-connected, best-recommended, best criminal lawyer in town. Everybody knew that.

Everybody knew, too, she wasn't going to practice law long. There was too much talk about ambassadorships or a place on the Oregon Supreme Court. Or, maybe in the governor's mansion or the senate. But Lydia wasn't angling for any of those highfalutin positions. She wanted to be a trial judge. She got it, too.

She had hardly closed the books on me before the governor appointed her to the circuit court. I think the only reason she took my case was because she wanted the inside gossip on Thaddeus's operation.

Her offices were on the thirteenth floor of a high-rise office tower in downtown Portland. Her card said she was on fourteen, but that was because the people who owned the building pretended there wasn't a thirteenth floor and called it fourteen, instead.

Part of me liked the idea of having a lawyer who presented her little corner of unlucky thirteen to all the world as if it were nothing less than the double sevens of the fourteenth floor. That was the go-for-it kind of attitude I wanted in somebody who represented me.

Lydia was tall and angular, and I could tell from the start that she was pretty sure I was guilty of whatever the cops thought I was guilty of. But whatever she privately thought, she was on my side. And, she was sure of her advice. "I wouldn't take that polygraph exam if I were you," she told me.

"I can do that?" I asked.

"It's called the Fifth Amendment." She relaxed back into her Queen Anne swivel chair, all smiles. "Protects you from self-incrimination."

I nodded, just as if I'd known that all along. Which, of course, I had. Even with all the classes I'd slept through in law school, I had watched way to many crime shows to let something like the right against self-incrimination get by me. It's just that, when it comes to your personal rights under the Constitution, you begin to lose confidence.

"So." Lydia steepled her elegantly manicured fingers. "Just what are you innocent of?"

"I'm not sure." That was another reason I had come to see her. I wanted to find out what the police had on me, and I'd heard she had contacts.

"Well, why do they want you to take a polygraph?"

"It has something to do with Thaddeus Silk, I think."

"They don't believe you murdered him?" Lydia looked at me hopefully. I think she would have enjoyed a good murder trial.

"I don't believe they think he was murdered at all."

"That would explain"—she laughed—"why I never saw any more about him on the six-o'clock news. So . . ." She folded her hands. "It's the missing treasure they want to know about." For somebody I had just met, Lydia knew an awful lot about my situation.

As fine a lawyer as she was, I was still a little superstitious about that thirteenth-floor business. When I thought about it, I couldn't see why thirteen was any less unlucky just because everybody called it fourteen.

"There was cash in the safe?"

"Four thousand nine hundred and eighty dollars," I said nodding. "In twenties."

"And passports and driver's licenses?"

I nodded a second time.

"Thaddeus!" She laughed.

"You knew him?"

"Everybody knew Thaddeus." She smiled, again. "Wonder what the bar is going to do with all the dues we pay, now that they don't have Thaddeus Silk to investigate anymore."

"They'll think of something." I was pretty sure of that.

"No *doubt*." She sounded pretty sure, too. "Anything else the police want to know about?"

"Engine Joe."

"Who's he?" She looked expectant, waiting for me to fill her in.

"I think he had something to do with the missing treasure. There wasn't anything in Thaddeus's client list on him. And no documents or anything else as far as I could see. But now . . ."

"But now"—she grinned—"you've found something you're not supposed to have. And you want to know what to do with it?" She seemed like a very experienced lawyer.

"This Engine Joe"—Lydia chose her words carefully—"what did you find?"

"A document," I told her, not really answering her question. "Thaddeus kept it in a dead file."

"So," she said, sounding stern, "*give* it to them."

"I'd rather not."

She sat back in her chair and smiled, waiting for me to tell her why I would rather not.

"I think he may be a client," I told her.

"Thaddeus's or yours?"

"My client, now. I inherited him when Thaddeus died." Then I told her what I knew about Grady Jackson.

"Put the document back in the file, then. And leave the file exactly where you found it. You don't need to get mixed up in any of Thaddeus's business." She made another note to herself. "You *sure* you didn't have anything to do with this?"

I shook my head. This business of trying to guess what the police thought they had on me was beginning to wear thin. "And I didn't steal any Spanish treasure, either. And I don't know anything about any fake passports or driver's licenses or why Thaddeus would have a stack of twenties in his safe. And *especially*"—the more I thought about it, the stranger it all seemed—"I don't know why the police would think I did."

In Europe, Lydia's office wouldn't have been on the thirteenth floor. It would have been on twelve. Over there, the bottom floor doesn't count. It's just the bottom floor. The first floor is a flight up, which means that, by the time you get to the fourteenth floor, you are fifteen stories in the air so, when you skip thirteen, fourteen drops back to the fourteenth floor where it belongs.

"I'll call the detective in charge and tell him there is no way you are going to take that polygraph." Lydia jotted another note to herself. "Later on, if we think it would be helpful, I can always set you up with a private polygraph. That way"—she put this carefully—"if something goes wrong . . . if the examiner is having a bad day . . . the police never need to know about it."

From the polished way she explained it, I could tell I wasn't the first client to hear this advice. But, still, if a private polygraph test would clear me . . . "Why don't I just go down right now and—"

"No need for that, yet." Lydia hit the speed dial on her phone.

A large, plastic M&M on the corner of her desk bounced on little spring legs as if agreeing that a lie detector was the last straw her clients grabbed at. I guess the idea that I might actually be cleared by a lie detector struck her as pretty remote.

In Japan, four is the unlucky number, so buildings in Tokyo skip the fourth floor and the thirteenth floor still gets called fourteen. It's five you have to worry about, because five is really unlucky number four. Of course, if a multicultural Tokyo building leaves out thirteen, too, twelve gets bumped all the way up to fourteen, and fifteen winds up on the thirteenth floor.

Lydia had a quiet conversation with somebody at the police department while I brooded over what floor she was on. My name went by a couple of times, but I couldn't tell what it was about. Then she listened for a while, said *hmmmm*, and listened some more.

The building she was in had a lower lobby and a basement beneath that. So the thirteenth floor would have been fifteen counting from the bottom. Except they would have called it sixteen, once the eleventh floor was renamed fourteen because nobody wanted to be on thirteen—which jacked the fourteenth floor all the way up to seventeen. Except, of course, in Japan, where it would have been eighteen if they'd been sensitive and multicultural and skipped thirteen, as well.

"They think Sophie was telling the truth," Lydia told me when she hung up. "They think there really was treasure in Thaddeus's safe. And they think you stole it. You really didn't take anything?" She looked at me skeptically.

"Of course not." I tried to keep my gaze as steady as I could. "Besides, if they think I robbed Thaddeus, why don't they arrest me?"

"Give them time." And then, she smiled to let me know I wasn't in that deep. At least, not yet. "They're not interested in what was in the safe the night Thaddeus died. They're interested in where he got what was in the safe. You *sure* you weren't in on any of that?"

"I only worked for Thaddeus for three months." I tried to think why that proved I was innocent. "He didn't know me well enough to trust me on any of his . . . whatever he was doing."

Lydia nodded as if that made sense. "Just don't give them any ammunition. And do not take that polygraph test." She gave me a relaxed smile, as if the whole tangle wasn't such a big deal. And, to her, I guess it wasn't. "One more thing." She leaned forward as I stood to leave. "They know you were in his office the night he died."

That stopped me in my tracks.

"They have the whole thing on tape." She tapped her legal pad. "They've had his office bugged for months. You'd better sit back down and tell me what went on in there."

Later, while I was heading down in the elevator, it occurred to me that, maybe, all that happens is that the elevator company skips thirteen because, even in this day and age, some people still get scared on elevators. So it's not the thirteenth floor that's missing, it's just the thirteenth elevator button. Like a lot of things having to do with the law, the whole question of which floor Lydia's office was on became so unnecessarily complicated that I never did get to the bottom of it. No wonder even lawyers have to hire lawyers.

11

SOMETIMES I WONDER whether Thaddeus suspected what was coming. That last evening in his office he sounded almost reflective. Or, maybe, it was the bourbon talking.

He pulled a bottle out of the safe when I came in and poured each of us a shot. "I have to keep it in there," he chuckled as he handed me one of the glasses. "Sophie has convinced herself that it's the bourbon that makes me not want to have anything to do with her. I think"—he tossed back his shot—"she confuses cause and effect."

Thaddeus slipped an accounting sheet he had been working on into one of the files on his desk. "Sometimes I think I should have stayed in Frenchman's Cove. Grady Jackson and I used to own a bar over there."

It was hard to imagine Thaddeus had started his career in a place like Frenchman's Cove. I'd driven through there a few times on my way down the Coast, but I'd never seen any reason to stop. Neither did most people.

"The Oregon Coast would be a beautiful place to live"—Thaddeus nodded to himself—"if you could figure out how to make a living. But I managed to scrape by. After a while, I had a few shekels saved up and Grady and I bought into the SurfSea together. I figured a bar would be just the place to shelter some income, if you get my meaning."

He gestured at my glass, but I didn't need another shot. He poured himself one, though. Then he set the bottle on the file where he'd put the accounting sheet. "That tavern didn't turn out to be the gold mine we thought. Too many details to take care of."

I wondered what kind of details he was thinking about.

"Distributors and that new sheriff, mostly. And some freelance interests you don't want to come down crosswise of." Thaddeus poured himself another shot. The bottle left a wet ring on the file when he picked it up.

"We knew about the poker game in back. That's one of the reasons we were willing to pay what we did for the place. The thing we didn't know until after we closed the deal was that, the first Saturday of every month, there was one special game, just between Sheriff High Hand and the owners after everybody else went home, and there would always be a lot of money on the table. Fact is, what was on the table was always one fifth of the take from the bar for the past month. And the sheriff would always get the high hand. So it was like we were all equal partners, fifty, fifty, twenty-five." Thaddeus set the bottle back on the file.

"After a while, these guys nobody recognized began hanging around. This was back in '71 and we had the only pay phone in town so, if you were expecting a call, the SurfSea was the place to be. People waiting for phone calls turned into a real profit center. And these guys were expecting a lot of calls. Then we started hearing about things going on out on the beach at night that Sheriff High Hand couldn't do anything about. All he would say was, it was way over his head and we'd better keep out of it. When you think about it . . ." Thaddeus turned his shot glass in the fluorescent light from the ceiling, as if he were examining the past through alcohol-coated crystal.

". . . the Oregon coast is just about the perfect place on the planet to bring in drugs. It's as remote as you can get and still be in the United States, and full of bays and inlets and hidden places nobody but the locals know about. And it's right next to Highway 101, so you can have your product to market as easy as if you brought it in through the port of Astoria. Anyway, whatever was going on with those guys hanging around the phone, the day came I didn't want any part of it and I pulled up stakes and moved to Portland . . . I kept a piece of the bar, though.

"For investment purposes." He looked wistful but, then, he'd looked honest and down-to-earth when we'd first met. With Thaddeus, looks didn't count for much where insight into the soul was concerned.

"I didn't need to be at the bar. Grady was the one who made it work. A man like Grady Jackson wasn't about to be intimidated by people hanging around to use the phone. He had that service forty-five of his." Thaddeus grinned at the memory and took another sip.

"Plugged a customer once, but nothing came of it. That was the advantage of having the sheriff as a partner. High Hand got to looking around and found out that the fellow had been running a pyramid scheme pretending to bring cheap silver out of Red China, and a lot of people had been burned. When he turned the shooting over to the grand jury, not a single juror voted to indict Grady and the whole thing blew over . . . Sure you don't want another one?" He lifted the bottle. This time I let him pour.

"All I do for the SurfSea anymore is handle certain delicate bits of advocacy . . . but the thing is"—he took another sip, and then let me in on one of the secrets of a successful law practice—"this particular type of advocacy . . . well, it isn't exactly law-school stuff. You have to learn it on your own, but it's the kind of thing keeps clients coming back."

They say every successful man has a mentor. I guess mine was Thaddeus Silk.

Thaddeus glanced around the office, as if noticing what his life had come down to. "Sheriff High Hand made a good partner for a cop and took care of us and kept us out of trouble with the law and a lot of other bad elements. But he overheated to death one New Year's Day in a sauna that an electrical contractor built for him after High Hand forgot to notice the electrical contractor doing ninety-eight in a school zone. First thing after the funeral, that New Broom Son-of-a-Bitch sheriff comes sweeping around, making a name for himself, and we have a new partner. Only his cut turned out to be a lot bigger, and he didn't even cover for us when those tobacco Nazis busted the whole bar for selling cigarettes to minors. You wouldn't believe how much special advocacy it took me to take care of *that*. And that wasn't the end of it. I had to advocate a whole new envelope full of reasons to that Son-of-a-Bitch New Broom to keep the law off our backs next time. But I did it right. Here's one thing you *got* to remember, lamb. *Mason v. Mason.*"

I must have looked blank. *Mason v. Mason* was one more in a long list of cases I had never heard of.

"Of *course* you never heard of it." Thaddeus smiled at the memory. "Never made it into the casebooks because Mr. Mason of the second part was too embarrassed to appeal." Thaddeus poured himself another shot.

"When I was a few years along, I represented Mr. Mason of the second part, which meant it was my job to respond to a petition for dissolution of marriage filed by Mrs. Mason of the first part. Started off routine enough, but by the time the hearing came around, a stripper named Begonia had figured out she wasn't in line to become the Mrs. Mason of the third part, no matter what promises Mr. Mason of the second part may have made to the contrary in certain unguarded moments, and young Ms. Begonia delivered to Mrs. Mason of the first part a whole box of tapes of late-night phone-sex conversations with the now thoroughly screwed Mr. Mason of the second part.

"Illegal as all hell, I thought, when the soon-to-be-ex-Mrs. Mason of the first part produced the tapes at the hearing. There is no way you can secretly record a private phone call and use it in court. Boy, did I think wrong, and those tapes cost Mr. Mason a bundle. So you just remember Mrs. Mason the next time somebody wants to ease the wheels of justice with grease he's asking *you* to smear around. You make your record just like you would in front of a judge."

The way Thaddeus explained things, being the pipeline for bribes, and then blackmailing the person you bribed with secret phone tapes, made as much sense as anything in the marketing books the Bar Association put out.

"You know," he said as he thought over what he had done with his life, "most things are temporary, if you wait long enough. But some . . . some things turn out to be . . ." He was the most melancholy-sounding man. "That Sophie is a geological feature." Thaddeus pushed back from his desk and rose shakily to his feet. "It's late."

He brushed past where I was sitting and put the bottle in the safe and closed the door. Then he walked back behind his desk and sat heavily in his chair. I guess going home took more energy than he could muster, that evening.

"Very late." And those were the last words I ever heard him speak. Thinking back, I'm not sure he was talking about the time.

There was something else I saw that evening, and seeing it was a pretty good reason to tell everybody I hadn't been there. When Thaddeus swung open the door of the safe to put away what was left of the bourbon, I got a look inside. There were bracelets and rings in there, just as Sophie had described to the police. And a couple of other rings, too, set with red stones that might well have been rubies, and a crucifix that looked like something a Spanish aristocrat might wear or, I supposed, the pope.

But, most of all, I remembered a small, gold brooch laid carefully on a piece of black velvet. What looked like an uncut emerald set in the center wasn't huge, the way Sophie claimed. But it wasn't small, either. And it looked old. It was exactly the kind of thing that might have lain buried on Neahkahnie Mountain, or under the sand on the beach, or in the water just offshore, for hundreds of years.

12

THE NEXT MORNING, I drove to Frenchman's Cove and picked up Abby. I wanted to meet the people who had been with her when she was arrested. The question I had for these guys—the big question—was, had she been selling dope at Rooster Rock? If she had, the district attorney was going to be able to prove it. And, right now—tomorrow morning—as soon as I got back to Portland—I was going to have to go to his office and try to cut a deal.

Abby directed me to an automobile repair shop in a sagging, two-car garage in back of a beat-up house on the Coast Highway. I don't think the operation was licensed because there weren't any signs out front. Abby's witnesses spread the good news about their business up and down the Coast to a select group of low-end customers by word of mouth. It was not the sort of place I would have been inclined to leave my car—especially if I'd had anything valuable in the trunk.

The first witness I spoke to had long, ropy muscles covered with tattoos, the face of a rodent, and was wearing a heavy down vest, even though it must have been eighty degrees. I got the impression he just hadn't gotten around to changing clothes since winter. The second guy was a huge, bearded biker. He must have been six-six, sported violet, wraparound shades, and had what looked like a pink milk shake painted on the back of his leather jacket. I have no idea what that was about. He also had, as it turned out, a sweet disposition, which might have been the result of all the dope he smoked.

Like Abby, both these guys stank of marijuana. If they showed up to testify, the district attorney would take one sniff, then spend a happy half hour educating the jury on the effects of too much THC on memory and perception. And Abby was going to go to jail. Which left her third witness as our best hope.

Shelley was short and alert with quick movements and bright, blue eyes. Whatever he was on, it wasn't marijuana. He was much too keyed up for that. And, unlike the other two, Shelley cared about things. He cared that the sheriff messed around with dopers. He cared that Abby had been busted. But, most of all, he cared about making sure the government left him alone. He cared so much I would bet he didn't have a Social Security number. Or a real driver's license. Or a permanent address. Or a telephone. Or a bank account. Or tax returns from previous years.

In Shelley's world, Pink Milk Shake and Ropy Arms weren't just a couple of worthless stoners. They were principled warriors for freedom—every toke a spark from the Flame of Liberty passed down from the Founding Fathers. And when they were around him, they believed it, too. And inhaled deeply and felt good about themselves with every puff.

Abby felt it, as well. Around Shelley she was no longer a burned-out firebrand of feminism, she was a Crusading Performance Artist for Freedom—a ribald commentator on the follies of government. That's what she had been doing at Rooster Rock when Deputy Bolt busted her, commenting on the follies of government. It hadn't been about dope at all. It had been edgy, in-your-face, politically based performance art. But it took a while to get that out of them because the conversation tended toward free association. After a while, I managed to ask the big question.

"*Sell* her shit?" Pink Milk Shake looked amazed at the idea. "*Abby?*"

"Yeah, man," Ropy Arms backed him up. "Her shit is *shit*, if you know what I mean."

"For sure," Pink Milk Shake agreed with himself. "Her shit is . . ." He groped for a way to express just how shitty her shit was. Then he found the perfect word. "Shit," he announced. "Her shit is *shit*. Out-of-*date* shit." He paused for another moment, trying to figure the best way to describe the out-of-dateness of Abby's shit. "*Bad* out of date." Pink Milk Shake giggled at how bad out-of-date Abby's shit was.

"Yeah," Ropy Arms agreed. "It's like something she found on the beach and just hung on to for too long and . . . and . . ."

The garage was a mess. Greasy auto-repair things were jumbled together on a wobbly card table shoved against the back wall. Lengths of bent wire were tangled up with tire gauges, a rubber mallet, worn-out spark plugs, a grimy air filter, two or three broken pairs of pliers, and a lot of other stuff I couldn't make out in the poor light. A custom-built .50-caliber rifle was in the garage, too. Shelley kept it on a tool rack to back up his beliefs.

"It's not just out-of-date shit," Pink Milk Shake was at his most eloquent, "it's . . . it's . . . shit! It's . . ."

"*Weak* shit," Ropy Arms looked thoughtful. "Out-of-date, weak shit."

"Like something people were smoking in the *seventies*," Pink Milk Shake elaborated.

"Yeah." Ropy Arms nodded wisely. "Like *seventies* shit. That's what it is, alright. Seventies shit. *Early* seventies shit. And—"

"Nobody *gives* a shit." Shelley gestured at the two to shut up.

After a while, the conversation wandered back to what had happened at Rooster Rock. "We were playing Attendant of the Opposite Sex," Abby said, as if that settled things. "I told you. We're performance artists."

"You were playing *what* of the Opposite Sex?" I wasn't sure this was leading anywhere I wanted to take a jury.

"Attendant," Shelley explained. "It's on the bathroom doors at all the state parks. *Here* . . ." He began rummaging through greasy car-repair things until he pulled out a small, blue-and-white sign. In the shadows, I could just make out the words:

ATTENDANT OF THE OPPOSITE SEX MAY ACCOMPANY OR BE ACCOMPANIED BY A DISABLED PERSON

"Sometimes"—Shelley smiled—"Abby will start feeling disabled and need an attendant of the opposite sex to accompany her . . ."

"And, sometimes, she comes down so disabled she needs *three* attendants," Pink Milk Shake agreed.

"Attend me," Abby moaned like an overweight royal, drooping her wrist into a fifty-five-gallon drum filled with trash. "*Attend* me."

"Those signs . . ." I tried to imagine how I was going to weave a defense out of stolen bathroom-door signs. "You want me to tell the jury that Abby stashed two and a third pounds of dope into her purse, then all four of you drove past—what? twenty?—state parks, every one of which is closer to here than Rooster Rock, and every one of which has the same signs on their bathroom doors, until you were at what just *happens* to be the biggest open-air dope bazaar in Oregon so . . . you . . . could . . . play . . . some . . . sort . . . of . . . *sex game* in the men's room? Is *that* how you expect me to keep Abby out of jail?"

"Of *course* they have the same signs at the other parks. So *what?*" Shelley's eyes lit up "The point is, they have them at Cock Rock."

"Cock Rock?"

"Sure, Cock Rock. Those pioneers were religious people." Shelley was dancing with enthusiasm—and, from whatever he was on, I suppose. "You think they could come across God's own hard-on and name it after a *chicken?*" It took me a while to realize he was referring to the huge basalt penis that Rooster Rock State Park was named for.

Loud clucking noises erupted from over by the tool rack. And, then, a cascade of giggles.

"They called it what it was"—Shelley ignored Pink Milk Shake imitating a chicken—"which is why it was Cock Rock all those years, and probably back a long time before that, too, because the Indians weren't blind, either. Then the goddamn government comes along and changes the whole fucking *thing* to Rooster Rock to spare everybody the humiliation of referring to it by the one word that pops into the mouth of every single human being who ever saw it. And the government gets all weepy about disabled people and puts those signs about attendants of the opposite sex on the bathroom doors, and—"

"And where would *you* go if you were into performance art? I mean . . ." Abby was on her feet, doing a jiggly dance of her own at the absurdity of it all.

"So, there you are," Shelley said quietly, "in a state park dedicated to a geological feature whose name you dare not speak, standing modestly at a urinal, rooster in hand, when an attendant of the opposite sex comes in and finds herself eyeball-to-eyeball with the very thing that cannot be mentioned. Now, you tell *me* you wouldn't pack up a few attendants of the opposite sex and motor on over to Cock Rock for a chance to—"

"And we could *prove* it," Abby broke in, "if that . . . that Deputy Bolt hadn't confiscated Shelley's movie camera. It was all *there*, and now we don't—"

"The DA's holding the film for evidence," I told them as I laid my briefcase on the cracked concrete floor, then squatted and opened it. It was a good briefcase, and I didn't want it anywhere near the card table.

"Evidence of what?" Shelley wanted to know.

"I don't think they've figured that out. The DA hasn't charged anybody with anything on account of it. But it was in the car, so it's evidence, and the DA gets to keep it. Like I said"—I pulled a reel out of the briefcase—"it's evidence. Which means we get to have a copy. You got a projector?" I was as anxious to see what was on that reel as Deputy Bolt had been when he'd confiscated the camera.

Pink Milk Shake and Ropy Arms rummaged in the farther reaches of the garage and came back with a projector. Shelley dug around on the card table and pulled out an extension cord spliced together with black tape. Then they set up a battered screen that had the collapsed look of a sail when there's no breeze. Nobody bothered to turn off the light, but it didn't make much difference. The light wasn't all that bright.

When Pink Milk Shake hit the switch, a hazy beam cut across the garage, the screen lit up, and Abby's voice began to crackle from the speaker.

Ding-a-ling, Ding, Dingus,

"Our Cock Rock poem," Shelley announced with the modest voice of authorship. "The disabled person reads it when the attendant of the opposite sex pushes her into the bathroom."

Dingle, Dangle, Dong,
Dink, Dang, Doodle, Wang,
Jing-jang, Ying-yang, Wong.

"Attendants," Pink Milk Shake corrected.

On the screen, an obviously handheld camera followed Abby being wheeled into a men's room. Inside, a pair of well-groomed young men in dark suits and white shirts saw what was coming and stumbled away from the urinals fumbling at their zippers. They looked like Mormon missionaries.

Big Bassoon, Bolt, Bamboo,
Dip Stick, Slip Stick, Sting,

You would never guess how many words there are for penis until you hear them spilled out one at a time like that.

"I mean," Shelley went on in the voice of the true believer, "why even call it Cock Rock? That whole cock business is nothing but—"

"*Regionalism!*" Abby piped up.

Regionalism? I hadn't been expecting that.

Dick, Wick, Swizzle Stick,
Joy Stick, Boy, Stick, Thing.

"Northern Regional Hegemonic Bias," Shelley explained. "Nobody from the South would ever name anything Cock Rock." He raised his fist in a sort of . . . I don't know. Not a black-power salute, that's for sure. But something radical or, maybe, reactionary. Categories got mixed up when Shelley was involved. "Sons of the South have dicks, not cocks. And other people . . . well, other people have other things . . ."

"They sure *do*." Abby guffawed.

Shelley gave her a you-would-know sort of look. "The poem is a multicultural expression of what Cock Rock could have been if the original settlers hadn't been so narrow-minded."

Lollipop, Lump, Lumber,
Digger, Dagger, Schlong,
Snake, Snack, Junior, Jack,
Plunger, Lunger, Prong.

There was a lot more along those lines, but it didn't get any better. Shelley was no Longfellow.

Listening to that poem, and looking at that movie, did not make me optimistic about Abby's prospects. I could use Ropy Arms and Pink Milk Shake as some sort of anticharacter witnesses, I supposed. The law library wasn't filled with precedents on the idea, but it seemed pretty clear to me that nobody could be more convincing on the one issue I hoped to make the centerpiece of the trial—that Abby Birdsong was such a world-class toker that she couldn't possibly have been planning to sell so much as a single seed out of her purse, because she needed the entire two and a third pounds just to get through the evening.

Which left Shelley as my fact witness. It would be his job to explain what Deputy Bolt had done to violate Abby's rights when he'd searched and seized her purse. Illegal search and seizure is the defense you always raise in these cases. As a point of constitutional law, it didn't make any difference how much dope she had been carrying. Or whether it was any good or, even, whether she had actually been planning to sell it. If the traffic stop wasn't legal, Deputy Bolt couldn't take the next step and look into her purse.

I would have felt better about what Shelley was going to say except, the more we talked, the more I was left with the feeling that he was looking forward to explaining the United States Constitution to the judge.

God save Abby Birdsong.

13

FROM ABBY'S, I drove up the coast for my first visit to Neahkahnie Mountain. Grady Jackson had invited me to spend the night at his house, and I was looking forward to meeting him.

The whole time I represented Grady, he never came to Portland, and he never, once, paid me by check. I didn't argue with either. I was always glad to get away from the office, and when I could work it in with a trip for Abby, I could bill both clients for the same travel time. And the payments in cash came in handy at tax time.

Neahkahnie Mountain formed fifteen million years ago from magma that spilled over the banks of a huge, inland sea of lava covering eastern Oregon and Washington, and southern Idaho. The molten rock flowed down the channel of the ancestral Columbia River in a cloud of fire and steam that must have changed weather patterns worldwide and was so massive that, four *hundred* miles later, when it boiled out into the Pacific, it was still plentiful enough and deep enough to form the 1,661-foot-tall promontory of Neahkahnie Mountain.

It's spooky up there. In the fog and wind, Neahkahnie Mountain is at the centerline of a band of storm fronts that circles the globe from west to east. Why this should be is as simple as it was mysterious before the advent of modern meteorological science.

At the thermal equator, the sun shines straight down, creating a band of warm, water-laden, rising air all around the world, but not much wind. Nowadays, we call this the intertropical convergence zone. The sailors becalmed there called it the Doldrums.

As the moist air rises, the pressure drops, and when the pressure on a gas drops, its temperature falls. That's how air conditioners work.

But, as its temperature falls, air holds less water, and the moisture over the equator falls back to earth to nurture rain forests from the Congo to the Amazon to the Celebes, Borneo, Sumatra, and the Malay Peninsula.

At the top of the troposphere, the now-dry air spreads out toward the poles, radiating heat until, around latitudes thirty north and south, it is cool enough to start sinking. As it loses altitude, the air compresses, and the compression makes it heat up, again. That's how a heat pump works. And, because hot air can hold so much more moisture than cold air, it is not only hot but dry by the time it reaches the ground. The result is that the hottest places in the world aren't at the equator, but in the bands of desert that surround the earth hundreds of miles north and south of the equator: the Sahara, the Sonoran, the Gobi, the deserts of India and the Middle East in the north, and the deserts of Australia, and Namibia, and the Atacama in Chile, to the south.

When the air reaches the ground, part drifts toward the poles, while the rest heads back to the equator to replace the rising air. Since the earth's surface has farther to go when spinning around the axis at the equator than at the poles, air drifting toward the equator finds the earth speeding up beneath it—which means that air that is doing nothing more than drifting north or south appears to move west, creating the trade winds that blow in continuous bands around the world in the tropics. The utter predictability of these winds set the shipping routes for the entire age of sail.

Air heading toward the poles finds the earth slowing beneath it and appears to blow from west to east. These westerlies are one of the reasons medieval Chinese junks and Japanese fishing rafts are wrecked on the coast of North America. They are also the reason that, for three hundred years, every ship from China or Japan or the Philippines wanting to sail to the rich ports of Spanish America had to cross the North Pacific to the California-Oregon coast, before turning south.

There's no place to shelter in the North Pacific, just cold and storms and endless, gray ocean. A sailing ship in trouble out there would have no choice but to deadhead directly east and try to beach itself before it sank. And, at forty-five degrees, right in the middle of the wester-lies, Neahkahnie Mountain stands like a beacon for damaged ships.

Since 250 years of these voyages took place before any settlers had arrived on the Oregon Coast, none of us, now, could know anything about it, except what we can glean from the bits that are left behind—the strange, evocative legends, the old maritime records, whatever we can find sunken or buried, or the mysterious carved rocks that have been showing up since farmers first began plowing the meadows south of Neahkahnie Mountain.

14

THE ROCKS WEREN'T all that big—a hundred pounds or so. Just the size for sailors to chisel capital *W*'s into. And capital *D*'s and capital *E*'s and things that might be Christian crosses. And, then, heave over and leave facedown in the meadow. Each rock also has a row of dots and an arrow with a feathered shaft, and, to this day, nobody knows what to make of them, except that they might have something to do with the stories the Indians told of pale-skinned strangers coming ashore to bury mysterious boxes.

Then, in 1869, a man named Hiram Smith found an entirely different kind of rock on Neahkahnie Beach. It had an angle of about fifty degrees carved into it and looked like something out of a geometry book. The more Hiram pondered that fifty-degree angle, the more convinced he was that he had stumbled across the key to the buried treasure. Thinking about that angle launched Hiram into one of the longest, strangest, and most tantalizing hunts for buried treasure in history—a hunt that had lasted a hundred years before it reached Grady Jackson.

They have a folder on Hiram at the Tillamook County Pioneer Museum. Inside are the names of his wives and children. They have a copy of his will and, even, a small photograph of him as a young man. He had dark, curly hair, a mustache, and the broad, agreeable features of an Irish bartender. For the rest of his life, whenever he could spare the time from farming, he trooped over the mountain and across the beach looking for the treasure he was sure was there. When he died, he passed the search along to his son.

Pat Smith started life with three first names—Patrick Henry

Marshall—because his parents couldn't agree on what to call him. Old Hiram wanted to name him after the firebrand of the Revolution, and his mother was a Marshall, so they compromised. They shouldn't have worried. Between them, they were to have thirteen more children—on top of the three already underfoot from Hiram's first marriage—and plenty of opportunity to exercise their nomenclatural yearnings.

There was nothing haphazard about Pat Smith. He prepared for a life hunting treasure as carefully as he would have for any other profession. He took correspondence courses in engineering to learn how to dig safely, and how to save labor. He studied the methods pirates used to bury treasure. He taught himself the trade jargon of the Indians of the Oregon Coast and, later, enough Tillamook to carry on a conversation with the locals—and with the woman he married when she convinced him she knew where the treasure was buried.

Since Pat thought the treasure might have been carried in a Spanish ship, he studied Spanish, and Portuguese, too. Then he traveled to Seville to search through the colonial archives. It couldn't have been an easy search. The Archivos Generales de las Indias must have been the most inaccessible depository of public records anywhere on the planet.

Nobody keeps records as carefully as a Spanish bureaucrat, and the archives contained eighty-some million documents from four hundred years of Spanish colonial rule. But they didn't have an index. And, they were only open to the public for a couple of hours a week, if *open* is the word. The statutes setting up the archives specifically stated that nobody was allowed to see any of the documents. Or be given any information contained in any document or, for that matter, any indication that any given document even existed. The only thing the statutes allowed was for "bona fide" interested parties to guess that a certain document might exist, then persuade a member of the staff to confirm that he had guessed right. And, if he had, to petition the Crown for a copy.

Somehow, Pat convinced the Spaniards he was bona fide enough to start the guessing game and, in a monument to human tenacity, made it back to Oregon with a list of seven galleons that had set out from Peru, loaded with silver. Of the seven, only five arrived at their destination, and one, according to the Spanish ambassador, was lost at Neahkahnie Mountain.

Pat's grit must have attracted notice because, after he came home, three Spanish engineers showed up in Manzanita with a map showing where the treasure was buried. And, just as Old Hiram had thought, the rock with the fifty-degree angle was the key. But, when the engineers offered to lead Pat to the treasure if he would show them where Hiram had found the rock, he turned them down because he thought he could locate it for himself. He should have been more forthcoming because, when he died in 1929, he had never found any gold.

He did find plenty of other things, though. One was a stone-lined drain sixty or seventy feet long and four feet wide, where an old Indian trail crossed Neahkahnie Mountain. A stream that had once run on top of the sand now flowed through the drain, and, to Pat Smith, this could mean only one thing—someone had diverted the creek in order to bury treasure in the streambed.

He found something even more suggestive. He found the wreck of an old wooden ship buried in the surf just off Nehalem Spit. From then on, he supported his treasure hunt by carving the ship's teakwood planking into walking sticks for tourists.

Even as an old man, Pat was tall and straight, his eyes clear and alert. It's easy to imagine him hopping around his digs with the quick, eager movements of a cartoon forty-niner. When he got past pick-and-shovel age, he took a man named Charlie Pike as a partner. Charlie set up a corporation and launched what the *Oregonian* described as "the best organized, most scientific effort ever made to unearth the treasure."

Pike built a power plant to provide water and electricity, and kept ten men digging an entire summer until they had a hole two hundred feet wide and from twenty-five to thirty feet deep. Then they used a diamond drill to bore into the bedrock. The whole time, a guard armed with a 30–30 rifle patrolled above, at least until the state police got wind of him.

When he turned seventy-five, Charlie Pike took time out to marry, but, the next year, he was back at work. He didn't have any more luck than Pat, though, or Old Hiram, and died in 1959 without finding any treasure.

15

AND, NOW, IT was Grady Jackson's turn.

After he was kicked off Neahkahnie Beach, he imagined the treasure he really wanted was hidden somewhere on the mountain. He imagined he knew how to find it. And he imagined people were shadowing him, trying to steal it. He was also very loud about it. That was the first thing you noticed about Grady, how much noise he made. When I pulled into his yard, it was raining.

Grady was back there, somewhere. I could hear him snapping branches and kicking through the undergrowth behind his house like an angry Sasquatch. "Goddamn *claim jumper*," he yelled, "get off my land," followed by the sound of a shotgun round being chambered.

I was beginning to think I had chosen the wrong client to spend the night with when he burst out from the trees. "You that lawyer?" he demanded.

From the stories, I expected him to be tall and lean, with the cool eye of Davy Crockett and the economical, easy movements of Jim Bowie. I was right about the tall part—and he may have been those other things when he was younger. But he was not young when I met him. He was seventy, I guessed. A heavy, old man with grizzled hair, a huge, flat face like a ham, and squinty pig eyes that made him look even more distrustful than he actually was.

"Well, come *on*," he yelled, again, when he had satisfied himself I really was that lawyer. Then lunged back into the woods.

Even without the noise, Grady wouldn't have been hard to follow. He was clumsy and slow and left big splotches every time he stepped in a puddle.

"Circle." He squinted when I caught up with him. "That's what you do when people want to know your business. Circle and circle and circle until nobody knows where they are, anymore."

He was wearing a black-and-red flannel shirt stretched over a bulging belly, khaki pants that looked as if they had come from an army-surplus store, a leather belt with a buckle made out of a brass horse-shoe around a silver dollar, and rubber boots. He had a twelve-gauge shotgun crooked in his right elbow, and, I didn't think about it until later, the flannel shirt was still relatively dry, as if he hadn't been outside all that long.

He circled us up the back side of Neahkahnie Mountain, through moss and ferns, making enough noise to alert every claim-jumper within miles to exactly where we were. "You just circle them to death. Circle and circle and *circle*."

Higher up, we came into a forest of enormous Douglas firs, climbing fifty or sixty or a hundred feet through dripping fog before the first branches jutted to the sides.

"I almost had it, you know," Grady told me in a whisper, as if he thought somebody might be trying to listen. "Only their supervisor walked off and they shut me down the next day."

"Supervisor?"

"Supervisor," he snorted in contempt. "That archaeology lady they made me hire. She said she was only required to be there for Indian artifacts, and lost gold wasn't Indian artifacts. Then, she went home and next day they kicked me off the beach. All she ever did was take notes. And talk. That woman could purely talk."

"I thought archaeologists were supposed to take notes," I replied. "I mean, wasn't that what you were paying her for?"

"Not those kind of notes. She wrote everything down, conversations, the places I dug, chance remarks. I couldn't move without her writin' her master's thesis about it. She claimed it was to make sure what happened in case of legal dispute." He grunted as he smashed through an unwary bush.

"I'll show her a legal dispute. All they really wanted was to get me

76

off the beach so they could have the treasure for themselves. I would have gotten it anyway, but the underwater channels flooded me out. They left underwater channels to protect it, you know. I hadn't dug more than a few shovels when the hole began fillin' with salt water." The way Grady explained it, the fact that a hole he dug on the beach filled with salt water was just more of evidence of how valuable the treasure was.

"Know what I found at fourteen feet?"

I had no idea.

"Gas. Like in King Tut's tomb. You tell me that doesn't mean something," he demanded, as if challenging me to tell him gas didn't mean something.

"The vault is a foot thick and the treasure is underneath. They lowered it down in cannon barrels. There's cedar boxes and metal chests, too. They've got religious artifacts at thirty-eight feet along with gold and jewels." Grady stopped and peered back through the shifting kaleidoscope of fog and trees, trying to spot whoever was following us. I couldn't see anybody.

"They're there, alright." He took a pull of bourbon from a thermos and started circling uphill, again.

As we climbed, the fog began to break and the trees thinned out. After a while, we came around to the ocean side of the mountain, the trees vanished, and the ground swooped away in a long, grassy curve, then plummeted to the waves crashing noiselessly below.

In the bright sunlight, we followed a narrow trail suspended a quarter of a mile above the surf, then back into trees and out, again, to look almost straight down at Neahkahnie Beach. For miles, the sand stretched away in a narrow spit between the ocean and Nehalem Bay, then down Nedona Beach and Manhattan Beach, until the view was lost in blowing mist. We were so high, it almost felt as if we could see the curve of the earth.

"Down there"—Grady pointed to a spot near the foot of the mountain—"is Beaver Pond."

I looked but I couldn't see a pond.

"It's marsh, now. That's what happens when beavers take hold of a stream. First, you get a pond. Then it marshes up. Later on, it turns into a meadow where elks come and lie down. I thought you city boys"—Grady gave me a look as if city boys didn't really know much—"watched public television." He took another pull from his thermos.

"Beaver Pond is where Mrs. Schmidt had her mystical experience with the bronze chest handles. That was in 1929, after she spent the summer at Manzanita taking the air and was overcome by a fit of restlessness . . ."

That was easy enough to imagine. Anybody who spends three months doing not much in a place like Manzanita is going to be restless.

". . . Only, Mrs. Schmidt didn't think she was restless because she was bored. It was a restlessness with a message, at least that's what her spiritualist told her." Grady shook his head at the strange things some people are willing to believe. "The message was to search the place where, on October twentieth, the rays of the setting sun were going to intersect the north-south line through the middle crown of the mountain." He passed me the thermos.

"Come October twentieth, Mrs. Schmidt had the north-south line all plotted, and surprisin' as it seems for that time of year, a ray actually broke through and landed on the exact spot where Sam Reed found the chest handles." Grady paused to let that sink in.

"But the ray was a little behind schedule. Nine years earlier, Sam had taken time off from bein' county commissioner and sent one of the handles to a museum in New York. When word got back it was Chinese from the late 1600s, people came from all over to dig up Beaver Pond. But nobody found anything, and Sam went back to commissionin' the county. By the time Mrs. Schmidt arrived, Beaver Pond was one of the most dug-up places in the entire state, and everybody knew there wasn't anything else there." Grady laughed. "Just goes to show what happens when people start believin' strange things."

Since that afternoon, I have clambered over Neahkahnie Mountain a dozen times trying to pin down where we walked that day. What I remember, besides the moss and the ferns and hiking back into the trees and down to his house, was an old, shored-up excavation. I didn't get a close look, but, at a distance, it appeared solid and the dirt looked fresh, as if it had recently been worked. I couldn't help thinking we might have walked past his private treasure hunt—the one everybody thought he had on Neahkahnie Mountain—but I never really knew.

Whether he even dug for treasure up there, I never found out. He had enough tools scattered around his yard to run a modest commercial mining operation, but they looked to me as if they were left over from when he had been digging on the beach. He had shovels and picks propped against the side of his house that seemed as if they had been leaning there for ages. Thick, wooden planks that might once have been used for shoring were piled in mossy stacks. He had a diesel generator and an electric pump and hundreds of feet of hose that could be used to drain salt water from a hole, I suppose. He even had a small backhoe half-concealed under a pile of fir branches. I didn't think about it that first afternoon, but the needles were brown, as if the branches had been lying on the backhoe a long time. None of it looked as if it had been touched in years.

16

"THE TREASURE," GRADY told me as we sat in front of his fancy, tiled fireplace that night, "is from the *Isabella*." Rain beat against the windows, and the room was drafty from the fire.

"She was wrecked in the 1700s. Just like it says in . . ." He looked at me speculatively, as if judging how much he could trust me with. "The key to the rocks," he said, "is in Second Samuel." It was dark in Grady's living room, with just a dim lamp in the far corner and the flames flickering in the fireplace.

"Second Samuel?" It was hard, even with Grady, to let such a remark pass.

"Yes, Second Samuel." And, then, he went on to explain—as if it all made perfect sense, "And, a little help from a certain monk who carved the rocks."

"Monk?"

"The one they held prisoner on the ship." Grady lowered his voice. "He made the carvings relate to Scripture, which is what gave me the key." Grady gestured to one of the Bibles on a coffee table, then sank back into his overstuffed chair.

"Once I had the key, there wasn't any doubt it was the *Isabella* Pat Smith found out there on Nehalem Spit. Or, maybe"—he looked thoughtful—"it was a pirate ship from the early 1600s." Grady didn't seem bothered by the idea of a ship in divine Scripture transposed into a pirate vessel from another century.

"The monk carved lots of rocks." He squinted at me in the half-light from the fireplace. "But I'm only usin' eight. The eight that were the cornerstones of the Temple of King Solomon."

"You have the cornerstones of King Solomon's Temple?" I asked idly. The bourbon was starting to take hold as I tried to imagine ancient Hebrews lugging cornerstones halfway around the planet to be carved with mysterious E's and W's and rows of dots by some kind of convict monk before they dumped them on the Oregon Coast.

"I don't have all eight." Grady's huge, flat face glowed in the dim light as he poured himself another shot. "I'm just workin' from *three*. The three," he said in a whisper, "that told me to begin diggin' at my own house and, then, work my way up the mountain. You know what I found in the yard?" he asked, jiggling with excitement.

I shook my head. I had no idea.

"An old Spanish flintlock, that's what. It's a sign." He stood and stepped heavily to the mantel and picked up a corroded metal tube. It could have been a four-hundred-year-old barrel from a flintlock, I suppose. I don't know what would be left of a gun buried that long. But my first guess would have had something to do with the sprinkler system the previous owner had installed before Grady had bought the house. And, then, I had another thought.

"What," I wanted to know, "happened to the treasure vault buried beneath the beach?" The one Grady had been so excited about that afternoon.

"There is more than one treasure," Grady answered darkly, "buried out here. What's under the beach, that's for children. The one I'm after is King Solomon's treasure."

He sat back down, then took another sip of bourbon. "I fixed that archaeology lady, too. I fixed her good. Want to know how?"

I nodded.

"I didn't tell her anything, that's how." Grady grinned, as if not telling the archaeologist anything was the best possible revenge.

"Nothing?"

"Not a goddamned thing. And, now, they're makin' their plans to dig down on the beach when the real treasure has been under the mountain all along." He leaned back and laughed at the foolishness of thinking something important could be buried under Neahkahnie Beach.

Grady's house had been designed by an architect. There were a lot of levels and lots of glass, and none of it went well with the Japanese/army-surplus/Victorian motif Grady had chosen for his decorating scheme. The house was crammed with low tables and overstuffed armchairs, and enough survival bric-a-brac to outfit a base camp for a treasure-hunting assault on Everest.

In the kitchen, ropes lay coiled on the counters, and lanterns and batteries were stowed in cabinets. The sideboard in a room the architect meant for formal dining was covered with trowels and rock hammers. Compasses and metal detectors and quiet, battery-operated power tools were scattered over tables and chairs, and, everywhere, topographical maps and charts and geological surveys were held in place by Bibles, and by the handguns Grady made a point of keeping loaded.

"It's these pistols," he'd told me after the first bourbon, "that keep my sister from visitin'. She thinks the house isn't childproof enough."

I thought his sister had a point. Grady Jackson's place was just about the most unchildproofed house I had ever seen.

"Came up here about ten years ago with her grandson. I guess he took after his uncle Grady because every time his flat, little feet hit the floor, he'd head straight for one of the pistols. Ellie said if I ever wanted to see her again, I was goin' to have to come to Tucson."

Grady nudged a Luger on the coffee table with his toe. "I thought I'd just wait until he got bigger, but it didn't work because she kept accumulating more grandchildren and there was no end to the two-year-olds. So I just go down there every winter to see her. Keeps her happy."

Grady chuckled. "Keeps me happy, too. Januarys and Februarys I sit in the sun and she brings me lemonades, and when she isn't lookin', I slip some bourbon in and teach whichever grandchild happens to be two at the time a little about gun safety. After a couple of months, I come home with a tan. Best way to spend winter on the Oregon Coast known to man." All of a sudden, keeping loaded pistols lying around where his sister's grandchildren could get at them didn't seem all that loony.

Grady had an enormous map of Neahkahnie Mountain and the nearby beaches pinned to the wall in his study. It was covered with red *X*'s showing where other diggers had tried their luck. Beside each X was a handwritten note explaining why that dig had gone wrong. Another map had mysterious markings Grady would not talk about except to hint they were the key to where King Solomon's treasure really was.

A third map spread across a large worktable may actually have had the treasure marked on it. I'm not sure, because Grady rolled it up when I came into the room. He wasn't giving away details, even to his lawyer. Maybe, when I thought about it, especially to his lawyer. The secret would be out soon enough, he told me. Once he had the treasure, he would tell everybody how he'd done it.

"Scrolls," Grady revealed in a low, excited voice as he rolled up the map. "Scrolls with hidden information about the future. And other things, too. Like"—Grady shoved aside a couple of Bibles and began to draw on the back of an old place mat from the SurfSea—"the location of lost mines and the Mystical Name of Great Power revealed to Moses on Mount Sinai."

His hand was shaking from excitement, and he had trouble controlling the pencil. Or, maybe, he was just old.

"Underground chambers," he whispered, and pointed to the place mat where he had drawn what looked like three igloos beneath the mountain. "Which proves why nobody ever found anything." He paused for emphasis. "The treasure's in underground chambers . . ." Then he put down the place mat and walked over to his desk and unlocked a drawer.

"There are other things, too. Important things I'm not at liberty to show you. But there's one thing, one little thing you can see." He pulled a Cuban cigar box out of the drawer.

Then he brushed aside what looked like an original Colt Peacemaker and set the box on the edge of the desk. He slowly opened the lid, as if something strange and wonderful were inside. And pulled out a small, blue medicine bottle he'd found under a patch of ferns, somewhere on the mountain. He wouldn't say where.

"This," he whispered, "is just one more sign." His voice trailed off in the semidarkness. "When those Spaniard engineers came out here to try to get Pat Smith to tell them where his old man found the fifty-degree-angle rock, one of them used to drink some kind of medicine, and I found his bottle. So, now, I know where they were lookin'." He closed the cigar box with an air of finality.

Grady Jackson had spent more than enough time alone on Neahkahnie Mountain to have gone completely insane. And that's where I would have left it, if I hadn't seen something else. Something I didn't think he meant me to see. It was a heavy, braided gold chain he'd swept into the drawer as he pulled out the cigar box.

The chain was long, maybe two and a half feet, and it spilled softly over the edge of the desk like a beautiful, fluid serpent glittering in the half-light.

From across the room, it looked as ancient as the brooch in Thaddeus's safe. And, a lot more valuable. It was hard to imagine where Grady, where *anybody*, could have gotten such a thing—certainly not an ex-bartender on the Oregon Coast who hadn't had any visible income for the past decade.

I wondered what else was in that drawer, but I never slipped back in to look. He'd downed a lot of bourbon by then, there were a lot of guns around. And, if there was any idea I did not want Grady Jackson getting, it was that somebody was sneaking around his house.

17

ON THE WAY into Portland the next day, I was pulled over by the police.

They claimed I'd changed lanes without signaling, and they were probably right. I'm famous for not signaling, but I don't think that's why they pulled me over. I think they saw me coming.

"You're the gentleman who doesn't want to take the lie-detector test," the patrolman announced when I handed him my license. "You got proof of insurance?" He was a pleasant-enough-looking guy with freckles and red eyebrows.

I handed my insurance card to him.

"Please wait here while I have these checked." When he stepped back to his patrol car and gave my license and insurance card to his partner, I stayed put. Portland cops aren't as high-strung as some police, at least if you're white. But it's a good idea to stay in your car.

After a while, he walked back over. "Mind if I have a look in the trunk?" he asked pleasantly.

"Mind if I see your warrant?" I asked back. With the time I had spent researching Abby's case, I was plenty au courant on the warrant requirement if the police didn't have probable cause.

"Velvet said you were lippy." He grinned.

Velvet? I thought. "You must have me mistaken for somebody." I didn't know any strippers.

"Nice lady. Blond. She and Rocco talked to you when that bottom-feeder lawyer showed up dead. Said you weren't very cooperative." He grinned again. In another setting, all that grinning would have seemed likable. "Betting down at the station is, you're the guy who made off with the treasure."

Ms. Good Cop's name was Velvet? I believed that about as much as I believed Rocco's name was Rocco.

"That treasure." He laughed. "I know we swore an oath and all. But I got to be honest with you, here. Checking every gutter and rat hole in town just to get a few trinkets back for somebody like that Ms. . . . Ms. . . . ."

"Silk. Sophie Silk."

"Ms. Silk. That's not something any of us are going to risk our lives over. We can let a thing like that slide forever, if we have reason."

For a moment, I thought he was asking me to supply him with an envelope of reasons not to arrest me for robbing Thaddeus's safe. But, that wasn't it.

"Now I can't speak for everybody"—he gave me a shy smile—"but I don't have to. Velvet and Rocco are the ones involved, and they are very good cops."

"The best." His partner had walked over to join us. He was a short man with lips like strips of bacon he was trying to conceal beneath a mustache.

"And they are very interested in getting to the bottom of just what was going on in Mr. Silk's office all these years," Freckled Cop picked back up.

"So, if somebody were to give them a helping hand, talk to them a little bit so they can get started," Bacon Lips chimed in, "then conscientious as Velvet and Rocco are, there are only so many hours in the day and they're going to find themselves way too busy to waste time looking for missing treasure."

My jaw almost dropped. These guys weren't asking me to bribe them. They were trying to bribe me. They were offering to let me keep the treasure if I would tell them what I knew about Thaddeus.

"I'm sorry." I shook my head and told them exactly what Lydia Stonemason had said I should say if the police kept pressing about the lie-detector test. "I just didn't work there long enough to know anything."

"We're sorry, too," Freckles told me. "We'd hoped you could help us put this whole matter to rest."

"We're not going to write you a ticket, this time," Bacon Lips said.

"Person with your record, we're just going to leave you with a warning."

"We'll be keeping an eye on you, though."

"To make sure you use that turn signal of yours." Freckles nodded, in the most pleasant, unthreatening sort of way. "You say hello to Engine Joe for us."

"We'll be keeping an eye on him, too," Bacon Lips finished up.

18

ABBY BIRDSONG WAS late for her own trial.

That was the kind of thing that would have been a problem in any other courtroom. At the least, the judge would have issued a bench warrant for her arrest. Then, when the sheriff dragged her in, there would have been a hearing for contempt—and, most likely—for flight to avoid prosecution, as well. But Abby seemed to move through life protected by the grace of some special dispensation. In the case of being late for her own trial, the dispensation turned out to be that none of us in chambers that morning had any idea what we were doing.

To be fair about it, Judge Wobberly, and the lawyer the district attorney's office sent to handle the prosecution, didn't know she hadn't shown up. I knew, though. And, worse, I didn't know why. She hadn't called from the side of the road with a broken-down car or given me any other excuse I could take to the judge. As far as I could tell, she really had skipped to avoid prosecution—only I was too naïve to know what to do about it so, in the pretrial conference when Judge Wobberly asked if we were ready to proceed, I told her we were.

After the conference, we walked into the courtroom and took our places, the judge on the bench, the guy from the district attorney's office at the prosecution table, and me, all alone, at the defense table. Looking back, you'd think that would be the kind of thing somebody would have noticed—the defense counsel sitting alone at the defense table. But the prosecutor was too busy studying his trial manual to spare much attention in my direction, and the judge . . . well, the judge was Doris Wobberly from probate court, and one thing about probate,

I guess, is you get used to proceedings in which the person of honor isn't there.

The prosecutor was tall, and a little heavyset, and wearing a new, expensive-looking brown suit. I think he bought it for Abby's trial. It was, I am pretty sure, the first case he ever prosecuted all by himself. Like me, he was cutting his courtroom teeth on a not-very-important criminal case.

I never found out for sure what Judge Wobberly was doing handling a criminal trial. I heard later that she had gotten old, and confused, and things had become so fouled up in probate that the presiding judge had pulled her out for a couple of weeks to let somebody else go down there and try to figure out what was going on. I never knew whether to believe that story—all I know for sure is that Judge Wobberly handled Abby's trial, then, two weeks later, disappeared back into probate never to be heard from again.

The first order of business that morning was selecting a jury. That was back when Oregon had some 220 excuses people could use to get out of jury duty, including having almost any kind of employment, from governor all the way to dog groomer. Which left housewives, retired people, and ne'er-do-wells for the jury pools.

My job was to get ne'er-do-wells onto the jury. A jury of ne'er-do-wells would be just the ticket for Abby and her dope-smoking witnesses. Ne'er-do-wells might even be willing to believe that what Shelley or Pink Milk Shake or Ropy Arms said made sense. Housewives and retired people, it seemed to me, were less likely to make that jump.

The trainee DA must have seen things the same way, because he used his peremptory challenges to get rid of ne'er-do-wells, while I used mine to strike solid citizens. Unfortunately for our side, there were a lot more solid-looking citizens on the jury panel than ne'er-do-wells, and I ran out of challenges a long time before he did.

The only other way to get rid of jurors is to challenge them for cause, which meant I had to show they were biased against my client. But even foggy old Doris Wobberly wasn't going to kick people off a jury just because they didn't like aging, hippie dopeheads—especially in a marijuana trial. All in all, the jury-selection system put Abby at a disadvantage.

One guy I especially did not want on her jury was an electrical engineer with close-cropped white hair, and a bolo tie with a moss-agate clasp. He looked like just the kind of person who would have strong opinions about somebody who smoked dope. I would have saved a peremptory challenge for him, but I didn't think I needed to. He was too far down the list to be a problem. Even if the trainee DA used all his peremptories and I used all mine, that engineer would still be the seventh person on a six-person jury—so I went ahead and challenged a kindergarten teacher, instead.

I counted right, too. Once we were out of peremptories, the panelists got seated, one after another. When we reached the electrical engineer, the seats were filled and he was left off the jury. Then, just as Judge Wobberly was thanking the remaining panelists and about to send them back to the waiting room, juror number four went into labor.

I guess it was the stress. She hadn't mentioned anything about today being her due date, but there she was—having her baby in the jury box.

Judge Wobberly was nothing if not gracious. She dismissed her on the spot. In the end, we wound up with three housewives, an elderly, retired carpenter, the lone, eighteen-year-old freak I was pinning my hopes on for a hung jury, and an electrical engineer with close-cropped, white hair and a bolo tie with a moss-agate clasp. I was worried about my freak. I could not imagine him standing up to those five other citizens, good and true, on a matter of dope-smoking principle.

Not that any of that was going to make much of a difference if I didn't come up with a defendant. Selecting a jury was one thing. You could overlook a missing defendant during jury selection. But there was no way I was going to get through an entire trial without having somebody notice Abby wasn't there. Luckily for my career, Judge Wobberly called a forty-five-minute recess before starting. Which gave me time to go find Abby. If I could.

I called her number in Frenchman's Cove, but nobody answered.

That was a good sign, I supposed. If she wasn't home, maybe she actually had set out for the trial. Then I took the elevator to the top of the courthouse and walked down, level by level, checking courtrooms. I had a fantasy that I might discover her sitting in the wrong courtroom, listening for her name to be called. But, no such luck.

Back at the defense table, waiting for trial to start, I was beginning to think this whole business of criminal-defense work was a mistake. Being disbarred wasn't exactly the career move I'd had in mind. Then, as if in some kind of horrible dream, Judge Wobberly gaveled the court into session and the trainee district attorney stood and began his opening statement without, even then, seeming to notice anything was wrong.

It was hard for someone who felt like throwing up to follow what the trainee DA was driving at, but I came away with the impression he wanted the jury to send a message to the people who haunt our streets that using an Oregon state park as an outdoor drug emporium to foist two and a third pounds of marijuana onto our children will no longer be tolerated in this community. He mentioned the thing about two and a third pounds more than was strictly necessary to convey the bare facts of the situation to the jury.

When he reached the part where he was supposed to make the jurors feel all warm and patriotic about sending Abby to jail, he turned to the defense table and stretched out his finger. "She"—he paused for effect—"she is the one who sells her poison to our innocent . . ." His voice trailed off as the thought came over him that he was pointing at an empty chair.

The trainee DA stood frozen for a moment, his arm slowly lowering to his side while Judge Wobberly leaned forward at the bench, looking as if she wanted to say something, but just what had escaped her.

If I hadn't known what to do before, I really didn't know what to do now. I shrugged my shoulders in a grade-school kind of way, as if Abby's not being there was a new one on me, too—as if she had somehow evaporated during the prosecution's opening statement. Then I closed my eyes, using the power of positive thinking to will her into the courtroom.

After a few seconds, I opened my eyes and turned toward the seats in the back, trying to convince myself she was sitting behind me, and . . .

THANK YOU, NORMAN VINCENT PEALE

. . . there, looking as if nothing unusual were going on, were Pink Milk Shake and Ropy Arms and Shelley and Abby Birdsong.

I had no idea how long they had been there, but it couldn't have been long. The trainee DA hadn't gotten more than ten minutes into his opening statement before the subject of Abby's presence at trial had come up.

I smiled and motioned to her, and she stood and walked to the defense table, dribbling a little trail of seeds from her straw bag as she approached.

19

SHE HAD ON a modest, seersucker dress and looked about as conservative and middle-class as you could want in a drug dealer. I think she imagined the vertical stripes made her look less fat, but, as an optical illusion, it was not a success. The stripes just made her look crosshatched, as if a cartoonist were trying to emphasize her lumpiness.

Judge Wobberly seemed to suspect something was not quite right about discovering the defendant sitting among the bystanders in the back of the courtroom, but she had been in probate too long to be sure exactly what and motioned to the trainee DA to proceed with his opening statement.

The trainee DA raised his hand and pointed at Abby and tried to pick up where he had left off, only he'd lost his place and had to put his arm down and back up a few pages to the part about sending a message to the people who haunt our streets.

When he had worked his way back to where he had been, he pointed at Abby all over again and accused her of being the one who sells her poison to our innocent children. It was the kind of thing that was more persuasive when directed at an empty chair.

Sitting at the defense table in her seersucker dress, Abby didn't look like the Menace Who Haunts Our Streets. She looked like a dumpy, middle-aged woman who wasn't a threat to much more than a ham sandwich—a dumpy, middle-aged woman dressed in mattress ticking but, still, not much of a Menace. She'd even put some makeup over the scar that ran across her eye. After a while, even the trainee DA realized the time had come to wind it up.

He sat down, and it was my turn. And I began a rambling discourse, explaining to the jury how there was more to the case than met the eye, and it would all be revealed in due course. Due course involved Shelley and Pink Milk Shake and Ropy Arms testifying to . . . well, they didn't really have anything much to testify to. But it seemed like a good idea to put on a defense, even if the defense didn't have anything to say.

My opening statement went pretty well. The jurors actually seemed to care. At least, the five solid-citizen jurors did. They sat upright in the jury box and looked my way and, sometimes, took notes on the yellow pads the county had given them. My freak was the only one who didn't seem to track what I was saying. He lounged back in his seat with a dreamy look, as if he wished he were the one who'd confiscated all that marijuana.

Then I began explaining that, no matter how much of whatever it was the sheriff thought he had found on Abby, none of it made any difference because she was just carrying it for her personal use and wasn't about to sell any of it. The way I figured it, five of those six jurors wouldn't have any idea how much one human being could smoke in a single evening, and what would take closer to a year to burn your way through. Unfortunately, I hadn't counted on the fact that one of the jurors actually knew a little something about marijuana.

"Are you shitting me?" my freak muttered in a voice loud enough to snap even old Judge Wobberly back to the present. "Two and a third pounds?" For a moment, my freak didn't look dreamy at all. He looked as if he was going to be the jury's expert on smoking dope.

When I decided I'd dug Abby's hole deep enough for one speech, I sat down and the trainee DA proceeded with his case. His first witness was Deputy Sheriff A. W. Bolt.

Deputy Bolt looked fine and upstanding in his starched uniform. He was clean-cut and square-jawed and straightforward, and if I'd been on the jury, I would have believed every word that was about to come out of his mouth. And, I was sure, a certain electrical engineer with close-cropped white hair and a bolo tie with a moss-agate clasp, and four other solid-citizen jurors, were going to believe every word, too.

One other thing about Deputy Bolt—he had been through this trial business a lot more than I had. Or, for that matter, than the trainee DA and Judge Wobberly and I had, all rolled together. I'd met him at the hearing on my motion to suppress, when I'd tried to convince another judge that the marijuana in Abby's purse had been illegally searched and seized.

Deputy Bolt had proved to be the master of the hearings process. He had known perfectly well that if he couldn't show he'd had reasonable cause to suspect Abby was using marijuana, then he hadn't had any right to search her purse, and the two and a third pounds of dope were not going to make it into evidence. And, if he let that happen, Abby would walk away a free woman, and he'd have one less greasy scalp to hang from his utility belt.

The moment Deputy Bolt spotted Pink Milk Shake and Shelley and Ropy Arms waiting to testify at the hearing, he knew exactly what they would say. They would contradict whatever Deputy Bolt said. As soon as he announced he'd had reasonable cause to suspect Abby had been using marijuana because she'd been walking funny, those goofs were going to tell the judge she couldn't have walked anywhere because she had been confined to a wheelchair. If he said she'd been slurring her speech, they were going to testify she was a nun under a vow of silence. If he said she'd been whistling old Creedence Clearwater tunes, they were going to claim she didn't know how to whistle.

So, Deputy Bolt did what he must have done at scores of other hearings. He came up with an entirely different reason to suspect Abby had been using dope. It was a reason nobody could argue with. He told the judge he suspected she had been using marijuana because he'd seen a glassy look in her eye. That's all he needed to do—claim he'd seen something in Abby's eye that made him suspect she was high—and nobody could say different.

Shelley and Pink Milk Shake and Ropy Arms sure weren't able to say different at the hearing, and the judge had hardly thought it over.

He ruled the jury was going to get to learn about the marijuana. And, with that ruling, the trial became a formality.

The trainee DA should have just shown the marijuana to the jury and rested his case. And the verdict would have taken care of itself. But he was new at the DA business, and the trial manual told him to present his case as a story. So, like any good storyteller, he started at the beginning—which meant Deputy Bolt wound up telling the jury about the glassy look in Abby's eye.

"Yes, sir." Deputy Bolt smiled at the jury. "Defendant had a distinct glassy look in her eye, which is why I had to search her purse." That was a nice touch, making it look as if it were all Abby's fault for making him do what he did. Then he went through the whole sordid story about what he had found in her purse, smiling at the jury the whole time. To hear Deputy Bolt tell it, it was a model arrest, an arrest that would be a case study at sheriff's academies all over the country from now on.

The jurors smiled back. Even my eighteen-year-old freak made eye contact with Deputy Bolt.

No way I was going to cross-examine that, and I passed.

Next, the trainee DA called a threadbare-looking botanist to testify that the dope was dope. I tried to cross-examine him, but he really was a botanist and I couldn't shake him out of saying so. And, it really was dope, and I couldn't shake him out of saying that, either.

Then he sat down, and it was my turn to put on a case, if I could. Which meant calling Shelley to the stand—not that Shelley had anything to say, but he was the best I could come up with.

Sitting in the witness stand, Shelley did not project the glow of easy familiarity with the truth that had surrounded Deputy Bolt. In fact, when I thought about it, Shelley was the one who looked like the Menace Who Haunts Our Streets. Maybe one eighteen-year-old freak would believe what he had to say. I sure wouldn't have. And, of course, he was Shelley, which meant he had his own opinions about what was going on.

Now plenty of witnesses refuse to take the oath, and courts have time-honored procedures to handle these people. But a witness refusing to acknowledge the authority of a court . . . with a single phrase, Shelley managed to turn himself from Abby's best hope for freedom into somebody who looked like a war criminal trying to pretend the International Tribunal at The Hague doesn't have authority over him. Except, war criminals dress better.

We had a little discussion at the bench about it. "What," Judge Wobberly wanted to know as she cycled through a momentary period of awareness, "is this guy trying to pull?"

"Nothing, Your Honor," I answered, glossing over that I had been wondering the same thing. "He's just a man who believes in personal freedom and . . . and . . ." It was hard to know what came after that last *and*, and I ground to a stop.

"Well," the trainee DA rescued me from the lost cause my line of reasoning had become, "if he doesn't acknowledge the authority of this court, then I see . . . no . . . reason . . . this court should hear his testimony." For a new guy, he was pretty quick on his feet.

"The point is"—I was still trying to come up with something that made sense—"the court doesn't need authority over a witness. The witness is only here to tell what he observed, and this witness will tell the court exactly that, just as soon as we end this distraction and I—"

"This is not a distraction, Your Honor," the trainee DA interrupted. "If a court doesn't have authority over a witness, it doesn't have authority over its own courtroom and—"

"I don't think it's appropriate to tell a sitting judge she lacks authority over anything in her own courtroom," I interrupted back. It had occurred to me that in Judge Wobberly's case, what made sense had nothing to do with the law.

"Counsel." Judge Wobberly glared at the trainee DA. "If you have any question about my authority . . . any question . . . at . . . all . . . now would be the time to clear the air." Old Wobberly may have been locked away down in probate for thirty-umpteen years, but there was one thing she wasn't going to tolerate, and that was a challenge to her authority. Not in her own courtroom, even if she had only borrowed it for a couple of weeks while the presiding judge got things straightened out downstairs. Not even if she hadn't quite followed what the challenge to her authority was.

Back at the witness stand, I had a quiet talk with Shelley about keeping his opinions on the government to himself, keeping Abby out of jail, and just answering the questions as we'd discussed.

And, it seemed to work—at least, for the first few sentences. When I asked what he had seen at Rooster Rock, he was clear and articulate and explained things the same way he had explained them in private. He told the jury that he and Abby and two others had been driving through the parking lot when a construction worker jumped in front of the car with a stop-sign-on-a-stick. And, then, Shelley started to freewheel. "He expected us . . ." Shelley's eyes lit up with the blue light they got whenever he was about to launch into some uncontrolled opinion on something involving the authorities. "He expected us to stop just like he was the—"

"And then what did you do?" I know it had been my question, but the time had come to cut him off. Three housewives, an elderly, retired carpenter, and, especially, a civil engineer with a moss-agate bolo and close-cropped white hair did not need to hear Shelley's opinions on who had the authority to direct traffic at Rooster Rock State Park.

"Well, like I say, didn't any of us see any reason a construction worker could tell a free American citizen where she could, or could not, drive, and Abby just kept on going, and first thing we knew, an asphalt truck ran us onto the curb, and then Deputy A. W. Bolt shows up and starts ransacking the car, so—" Shelley had circled around and we were safe on base, talking about the drug bust.

"Did Deputy Bolt ask permission to search the car?"

"Of course not." Shelley breathed contempt. "He just ordered us onto the street and began going through our stuff. Then the next thing we know, he's got Abby's purse and is going, 'My, my, my, what have we here?' And he never did anything about that guy impersonating a police officer." Shelley glared at Deputy Bolt, sitting in the back of the courtroom. "I guess he didn't have a quota on construction workers."

That seemed like a really good time to get Shelley off the stand, so I said, "No more questions," and thanked him. Unfortunately, that just gave the trainee DA the chance to cross-examine.

"So, if I remember correctly," the trainee DA asked Shelley, "you testified that Ms. Birdsong was driving through the parking lot at Rooster Rock State Park when an asphalt truck forced her to the side of the road?"

"Yes." Shelley smiled. "An asphalt truck driven by another construction worker."

"And, what were construction workers doing out there that afternoon?"

"You mean besides harassing honest citizens?" Shelley asked back.

"I mean, what kind of construction work were the construction workers doing?"

"Paving." Shelley folded his arms.

"Paving what?"

"The parking lot," Shelley muttered. He could tell where this was going.

"The parking lot?" the trainee DA said in his best, most astonished voice. "The construction workers were paving the very parking lot at Rooster Rock State Park that defendant Abby Birdsong was trying to drive through?"

Shelley nodded, gloomily.

"Let the record reflect the witness indicated agreement." The trainee DA grinned his best Clarence Darrow grin at the jury. And, then, back to Shelley. "So, when the asphalt truck forced Ms. Birdsong to the side of the road, it was really protecting her from driving through newly laid asphalt?"

"What it was doing," Shelley said, trying to steer the cross examination back to where it was supposed to be, "was interfering with the rights of an American citizen under the cover of some kind of pretend police authority that a construction worker does not have."

"Unfortunately"—the trainee DA didn't sound as if he thought it was unfortunate at all—"the construction worker is not on trial here." This guy was handling himself so well I was starting to wonder whether he might be some kind of ringer. Then he asked Shelley what Abby had been doing at Rooster Rock if she hadn't come to sell dope.

One of the things they try to impress on you in law school is, if you have something embarrassing in your case, bring it out, yourself. It's going to sound a lot more embarrassing if you let the other side bring it out. That would have been good advice to remember. Instead, I'd skipped that very question on the hope that the trainee DA wouldn't care why Abby had been at Rooster Rock. Unfortunately, he seemed pretty set on finding out.

"Were you swimming?"

"No." Shelley shook his head.

"You mean to tell the jury you drove from Frenchman's Cove all the way to Rooster Rock State Park, and you didn't go swimming?" This was for the solid citizens on the jury. There is only one reason a carload of people would hang around a nude beach if they didn't want to swim, and that was to ogle other people swimming. And, if there was one thing an electrical engineer and three housewives and, likely, an elderly, retired carpenter might disapprove of more than swimming without your clothes on, it was sneaking around, spying on other people swimming without their clothes on.

"And"—the trainee DA grinned—"did you have a movie camera with you?"

"Yes." Shelley nodded.

"And the reason you had the movie camera"—the trainee DA closed in for the kill—"was to take porno movies of people swimming nude?"

It turned out there actually was one thing solid-citizen jurors might disapprove of more than sneaking around, spying on people swimming without their clothes on, and the trainee DA had found it. After that, it didn't make any difference what Shelley answered. The jury was thinking naked people, and pornography, and dope dealers. And, Abby Birdsong was at the bottom of it all.

By now, the trainee DA had scored just about every point there was to score. It would have been a good time to sit down, shut up, and wait for the guilty verdict. But he didn't have it in him. That was his flaw as a lawyer, and when Shelley denied making porno movies, he couldn't resist asking what the camera had been for.

"Performance art," Shelley told him. "We were being attendants of the opposite sex."

"Attendants of the opposite what?" The trainee DA hadn't been expecting that.

"Attendants of the opposite sex." Shelley pulled a crumpled piece of paper from his shirt pocket.

"What, exactly," the trainee DA demanded, "are attendants of the opposite sex?"

"Attendant of the opposite sex"—Shelley glanced at the paper to be sure he got the wording right—"may accompany or be accompanied by a disabled person."

There was something about that paper . . . the trainee DA scowled, trying to remember what he had heard about papers in law school. And, then, he had it. "Are you using whatever is on that paper to refresh your memory?"

"Yes," Shelley answered, "I want to get it right."

"Your Honor." The trainee DA turned toward the bench. "I believe that, under the rules of procedure, when a witnesses uses a document to refresh his memory, opposing counsel may require that the entire document be read into the record."

"Objections?" Judge Wobberly turned to me.

For all I knew, there may well have been some objection to that. But, since neither I nor the judge would have had any idea what, I let it slide. "No, Your Honor." It wasn't until a couple of days later that it occurred to me to wonder just how many trials Shelley had been involved in. And, whether he'd already known about the rule requiring him to read the entire document into evidence.

"Here." He tried to hand the paper to the trainee DA. "Read it yourself."

The jurors stared in fascination. They knew strange things went on at Rooster Rock. And, now, they were about to find out what those strange things were.

"No." The trainee DA refused the paper. "You read it. Just read to the jury exactly what it says." I was starting to have a bad feeling about what might be on that paper.

"Very well," Shelley began. "Attendant of opposite sex may accompany or be accompanied by a disabled person." Then, he began to recite the Cock Rock poem.

"Ding-a-ling, Ding, Dingus,

"Dingle, Dangle, Dong,

"Dink, Dang, Doodle, Wang,

"Jing-jang, Ying-yang, Wong."

"What?" the trainee DA interrupted. "Is that?"

"Please read back what I just said." Shelley grinned at the reporter. Evidently he had been in court a few times.

"Ding a ling ding dingus dingle dangle dong dink dang doodle wang jing jang ying yang wong," the court reporter read without much poetic feeling. She was a prim-looking, older lady with gray hair pulled back in a bun.

"Now, if you don't mind, I will finish it." Shelley was having trouble keeping his hands from shaking, he was so revved up. But he rose to the occasion. From "Mansicle, Meat, Muscle" all the way through to the boisterous, upbeat "Joy Stick, Boy, Stick, Thing," he read the poem with so much pride he could have been Alfred, Lord Tennyson reciting "The Charge of the Light Brigade" to patriotic English ladies over tea.

"Is there any reason"—Judge Wobberly glared over the bench when Shelley had finished—"I shouldn't hold you in contempt?" She would have been livid if it weren't for the blushing.

"Just one," I answered before Shelley had the chance. "Counsel specifically ordered the witness to read the document. If there is any contempt around here, it is not the witness's." Technically I wasn't Shelley's lawyer, but nobody seemed to care.

Judge Wobberly turned her glare onto the trainee DA, but nothing came of it. I think they were both too embarrassed to follow up on what had just taken place. After a while, the trainee DA said, "No more questions," Shelley stepped down from the stand, and that was that.

I wish I could say that what happened next was because of good lawyering on my part. But the truth is, my witness list had fallen apart and there wasn't anything I could do about it. I had meant to call Pink Milk Shake and Ropy Arms to further illuminate matters for the jury, but when I turned around, Pink Milk Shake wasn't in the courtroom. And, neither was Ropy Arms.

I asked for a ten-minute recess and fanned out over the courthouse, again, but they were nowhere to be found. In the end, I didn't have any choice but to rest Abby's case without ever putting on any evidence about how much dope she could smoke in a single evening. So much for trial strategy.

I found out later that, while the trainee DA and I were arguing about whether Shelley was subject to the jurisdiction of the court, the bailiff had walked over and ordered Ropy Arms and Pink Milk Shake to stand the fuck up and show some respect when the judge entered the courtroom. Then all three had stepped into the hallway to discuss the niceties of judicial etiquette.

In the hall, Ropy Arms had leaned into the bailiff's face and pointed out that since neither he nor Pink Milk Shake were citizens of Multnomah County, Judge Wobberly wasn't in charge of them and they didn't have to do anything about her one way or another.

The bailiff wasn't as mean-looking as Ropy Arms, but he was armed, and he leaned back into Ropy Arms' face and pointed out that he didn't give a shit what goddamn county they lived in, when they were in his court, they would show respect to the motherfucking judge.

Pink Milk Shake tried to calm things down by pointing out that he, Pink Milk Shake, and Ropy Arms were members of a religious sect that frowned on standing in the presence of people in robes.

The bailiff was nowhere as big as Pink Milk Shake, but he was still armed, and he pointed out that Pink Milk Shake was a cocksucking liar, and that's when the shoving started. Luckily for the cause of domestic tranquillity, a couple of other bailiffs happened to be passing down the hall at the time, matters got cooled off, and all that happened was that Pink Milk Shake and Ropy Arms found themselves on the street with instructions never to bring your sorry-assed butts back in my courthouse again.

That would have been another really good place for the trainee DA to shut up and go back to his office a winner. Instead, he told himself that Shelley needed rebutting, and he blew the entire trial by calling Deputy Bolt back to the stand to tell his tale all over again.

Deputy Sheriff A. W. Bolt started back at the part about how he had "observed a glassy look in defendant's eye," and all six members of the jury smiled as eagerly in his direction as they had the first time around. It almost seemed comforting, like children at bedtime listening to the same, beloved story they heard every night.

"So," the trainee DA bored in, "a glassy look is typical of—" He never finished the question because he was interrupted by a rattly sound coming from the defense table.

While everybody else had been flirting with Deputy Bolt, Abby had popped her glass eye onto the counsel table and, in a swirl of seersucker, was rolling it around like a marble, as if it had just occurred to her that she had a glass eye. Which it probably had, or she would have popped it out the first time Deputy Bolt had testified.

That was what the scar across her forehead and her cheek turned out to be about. The choker cable that had snapped up and hurt her back had caught her in the face, too.

It took the jury about fifteen minutes to come back with a not-guilty verdict. When they did, they had a retired electrical engineer with close-cropped white hair and a bolo tie with a moss-agate clasp as their foreman to deliver it.

And, that was that. Judge Wobberly couldn't even fine Abby the $500 for possession for personal use—the jury had found her not guilty of anything. The trainee DA was game, though. He tried to get her on a traffic infraction. She had admitted to that in open court. Surely a new trial on that crime was in order? But, even that didn't fly.

Before I could stop her, Abby pulled her *Oregon Driver Manual* from her purse and handed it to Judge Wobberly. Then the judge and the trainee DA spent ten minutes brushing seeds from the pages while they flipped from section to section trying to pin down exactly where it said a driver had to obey a construction worker. When they gave up, Judge Wobberly thanked the jury, retired to her chambers, and Abby walked out of the courtroom a free woman.

Two weeks later, Judge Wobberly disappeared back into probate, never to be seen again.

20

A **FEW DAYS** after the trial, I got a call from K. C. Thatcher. She was the manager of a radio station in Blythe, Oregon. I can't remember the call letters, but it billed itself as the Spirit of Yamhill County. My victory in the Great Rooster Rock State Park Drug Bust trial had made me famous—or, at least it was going to, just as soon as K-Something had me on their Friday call-in show.

I had never been to Blythe, but I knew it was a few miles west of Elk Prairie. The sign on the Interstate said so: NEXT EXIT ELK PRAIRIE— BLYTHE.

Friday morning, I gave myself forty-five minutes to get there. Forty-five minutes, I calculated, would put me at the station with plenty of time to meet the host and make myself comfortable before going on the air. What I didn't calculate on was getting stuck behind a semi filled with discount furniture.

It was slow going, creeping along behind that furniture, but it was a pretty day and I had plenty of time to make it to Blythe, introduce myself at the station, and get situated for the admiring audience of rural marijuana fanciers—that is, until about twenty minutes before showtime when we came to a road sign that made me realize the limits of my sense of geography: BLYTHE 26 MILES.

Fast as I was going when I finally got by that truck, I may actually have made it to K-Something by showtime—I'm not sure, because it never crossed my mind that I might pass it on the way into town. So, by the time I stopped to ask directions, turned around, sped back the other way, spun into the lot, and dashed inside, I was ten minutes late.

Or, as it turned out, twenty minutes early.

"We tell *all* our guests the show starts half an hour before it really does," K. C. Thatcher told me. "For some reason, everybody thinks Blythe is just this side of Elk Prairie, except"—when she thought about it—"that professor from Mt. Hood Community College. We found him asleep on the steps at five thirty one morning when we opened up." K.C. may have been the most beautiful woman I ever personally met.

She pointed out the host of the show. He was on the other side of a glass panel in the broadcast booth, and I began to wonder just what went on in these rural radio stations. He looked like Pink Milk Shake and Ropy Arms hand-rolled into one, he was so ostentatiously into blowing dope. Or, more likely—blowing up power stations.

At a guess he was twenty-five, and a Shining Path terrorist. He looked half–South American Indian, half-conquistador, had long, greasy hair, and wore a beat-up army field jacket he'd boosted from a Goodwill, somewhere. Part of me suspected that, if I went into the booth with him, I wasn't coming back out—held hostage while he broadcast his list of nonnegotiable demands to the fascist, exploitative, patriarchal government of Yamhill County. At least, I thought to myself, I was wearing my camel sports jacket, so the SWAT team wouldn't mistake me for him when they came blazing through the walls with their belt-fed shotguns.

"Why don't you hang that jacket over there?" K.C. gestured to a hook on the back of a door. "Then you can step into the booth and get acquainted with the host." I did just as she said. I put my jacket on the hook and stepped into the booth. K.C. got a lot of mileage out of being so good-looking.

When he spoke, the host didn't sound like somebody who spent his nights blowing up power stations in the name of indigenous peoples. "It's an hour show," he told me in an elegant, snooty, public-radio-classical-music sort of voice. "I will give out the station's phone number from time to time so people can call. But you must understand we are a long way out in the country, and most of our listeners don't have phones in their combines, so don't expect much."

"Nobody ever calls," K.C. agreed from the doorway.

"Except for that show we did on phonetics," the host went on. "People were stopping alongside the road at phone booths, they were so excited."

"We're going to have to do another one like that." K.C. jotted a note to herself on a little pad. "You don't think you could work something about fricatives or off-glides into the story about the trial, do you?" She eyed me speculatively, and, for a moment, I was tempted to change the entire history of what had happened in court.

The host turned out to be a wonderful interviewer filled with insightful questions. He asked about Abby and the Fourth Amendment and jury selection, then followed up with new questions based on what I answered. He made me feel I had done something remarkable and important, and the show sailed along. Whether we had any listeners, though, wasn't at all clear until, about forty-five minutes in, when we got a call that left both of us baffled for something to say.

I think if he'd had more experience with callers, the host might have pulled the plug. As it was, we sat and listened to a marijuana-befuddled voice running on about the one question I had never been able to answer about Abby Birdsong. "I know where she made her score, man."

I wasn't sure I wanted to find that out—at least not over the public airwaves from some toked-up stranger.

"It was on the beach. She ripped it *off*, man." The voice kind of giggled. "She's lucky to be alive."

The host and I glanced at each other, but he still didn't hang up.

"This huge pile of shit disappeared right behind the dunes." The voice giggled, again. "And the real owners never found out where it went."

I didn't know whether I was supposed to take Abby's side or keep my mouth shut or say no comment. Nothing like this had ever happened to me, before. Besides, I wasn't even sure I was her lawyer, anymore. The trial was over, after all. Then, the caller lowered his voice. "People were looking for that stash, if you get my meaning."

In law school, we spent a lot of time in ethics class discussing a gentleman from St. Louis named Caterpillar Haines. Caterpillar had more hands out than a politician, but he made his real living as Legal Champion to the Drug Dealers. "Even the worst criminals deserve good representation," Caterpillar would announce at a press conference whenever he was about to crank up his billing machine to siphon off drug money from another high-profile, worst criminal who was in immediate need of good representation.

The problem with Caterpillar was that his representation was too good. It seemed like all a criminal had to do was pay Caterpillar enough drug money and, the next thing you knew, the judge or the prosecutor or, once, even the governor would conclude that Mr. Criminal had wrongly been arrested, or that his heart was too weak to stand trial, or a juror would get it into his head never to vote for conviction, no matter what the evidence showed, and one more worst criminal would walk out the front door of the courthouse and back to doing whatever it was he had been doing to get himself arrested in the first place.

"I know what I'm talking about, man," the caller almost whined, as if he were used to not being believed. "Me and Abby, we were an item." Then he hung up.

The host switched off the mike. "Every station gets cranks like that," he told me in deep, rounded tones, as if he were announcing Köchel listings to classical-music lovers. "The only thing they really know is that the computer chips the Martians planted in their brains made them call." Then he laughed and switched the mike back on. And gave out the phone number of the station one more time, in case anybody else with computer chips in their brain had opinions on Abby Birdsong and the huge pile of shit that had disappeared right behind the dunes, man. But, nobody did, and the show wound up.

What concerned me was that the real owners might still want the dope back. And who, exactly, listened to Friday-morning call-in shows in Yamhill County.

I didn't want anything to do with drug dealers. It had been a simple malpractice claim asserted outside the usual channels, after all, that had brought Caterpillar Haines's career to a sudden conclusion.

Even Caterpillar couldn't win them all, and the day came when nobody in authority decided that his hot-shot client had wrongfully been arrested, or that the particular heart in question was too weak to stand trial, and the jurors were sequestered in a secret motel, so none of them came up with the notion to never vote for conviction no matter what the evidence showed, and, after trial, instead of strolling out the front of the courthouse in a $4,000 suit, Caterpillar's client shuffled out the back, chained to a one-eyed pimp with a gold tooth and a bad case of the jitters from heroin withdrawal. The following evening when Caterpillar stepped outside his office into a spray of machine-gun bullets, an interesting example for law-school ethics classes took an entirely new turn.

Before I could decide whether it would be a good idea to vary my own office hours, K.C. slipped into the broadcast booth and threw her arms around me. "Great interview," she said. She even sounded as if she meant it.

I was stunned all over again at how gorgeous she was. "What," I asked, "does *K.C.* stand for?"

"Killer Chick," she said, and bounced out of reach.

21

BACK AT THE office, Tail Pipe was confessing his sins when the Department of Justice called. He had reached Step Five down at Alcoholics Anonymous, and the time had come to admit to God, to himself, and to another human being the exact nature of the wrongs he had committed. For the human being to admit to, he chose Jolene.

Personally, I don't think he had a lot to confess. From what I could tell, mostly he just felt bad about making it home alive from Vietnam. Jolene was sweet about it, though. She sat quietly at the reception desk, reading a history of Sir Walter Raleigh's expedition to the Orinoco River while Tail Pipe ran through an endless list of wrongs nobody else would have felt guilty about. Every now and then, she would set down the book and come over and put her arm around him. After he was comforted, she'd go back to the reception desk and start reading, again, while he searched the shadows in his head for more memories of wrongs that were all his fault. This qualified as a busy morning.

The reason the Department of Justice called was to offer Grady and me a deal: our freedom in exchange for the treasure. It was the kind of offer that might have appealed to anybody but Grady. "Look," the lady said quietly when I picked up the phone, "here's what happens." She had a deep voice that made her sound almost like a man. "Mr. Jackson turns over everything he's dug up over the years, you give us whatever artifacts happen to have found their way into your safe-keeping, we forget about the Sunken Treasure Act, and this whole thing blows over."

Sunken Treasure Act? I was dumbfounded. Here I was worried about being gunned down over some huge pile of shit Abby had ripped off from right behind the dunes, man, and the Department of Justice was threatening Grady and me with prosecution under some kind of sunken-treasure law?

"In the first place"—I tried to make my voice sound as deep as hers—"the police and the Bar Association both went over this office after Mr. Silk died, and there wasn't anything here. And, in the second place, I've spoken to the archaeologist who worked with Mr. Jackson and she . . . everybody . . . says the same thing, that he never found any treasure out there, so, unless the state wants to confiscate a section of old sprinkler system that came out of his yard, there's nothing to turn over."

"Let's just say," the lady from the Department of Justice just said, "that whatever that archaeologist may have told you, we think your client found something. And we think," she said slowly so I would be sure to understand what the Department of Justice thought, "he has been . . . disposing of it . . . through . . . your . . . office. So"—her voice turned deeper and more threatening—"whatever happened to be in Mr. Silk's safe the night he died, or didn't happen to be there, either one, we want it back. So, what you need to do, Mr. Lawyer"—the way she said *mister* did not sound all that respectful—"is have a very serious talk with your client before we run out of patience. We won't be making any more offers."

I had the serious talk, of course. As Grady's lawyer, I didn't have any choice. But there was no way the State of Oregon, or his lawyer, either one, was ever going to talk Grady Jackson into doing anything he hadn't already made up his mind to do.

And as for me, well, I wasn't sure what to do. I called Lydia Stonemason, and she told me that if the DOJ really had anything on me, they wouldn't be trying to deal. That the best thing for me to do was just hang tough and wait for their next move. We could handle it when the time came.

Easy for her to say.

22

WHILE I WAS hanging tough waiting for the DOJ to make their next move, I found out who it was that listened to Friday-morning call-in shows in Yamhill County. It was the landlord of Abby Birdsong's storage locker.

Abby phoned from the Siletz County Jail about it. She had been busted for possession for sales, but, this time, it wasn't over a rinky-dink couple of pounds in her purse. This time, the sheriff had found the four and a half tons in her storage locker, and, suddenly, I was representing the biggest big-time drug lord ever taken down in Siletz County. Probably, on the entire Oregon Coast.

A lot of people wouldn't have cared about some incoherent babble on the radio, but the landlord of Abby's storage locker wasn't a lot of people. He was an elder in the Presbyterian Church. He must have been interested in phonetics, too, because he'd turned on his radio just in time to hear a dopehead running on about Abby and her huge score. The man didn't even drink wine, but he knew about dope. It had only been a couple of weeks since he and the rest of the Elks had toured the sheriff's office and been introduced to a brick of marijuana that had been confiscated at Cape Kiwanda State Park. And dope wasn't just at Cape Kiwanda, the deputy told them. It was all over the Oregon Coast. Just like in the early seventies.

Nobody had a particularly good fix on what had really gone on in the early seventies. Back then, a lot of people thought the talk about drug smuggling had been blown out of proportion. But how could you ever know? Something had been happening out on the beaches at night. Most likely, it was just kids passing around bottles and talking big.

Other people weren't so sure. There had been too many rumors about boatloads of drugs coming ashore and strangers hanging around the SurfSea Tavern waiting for phone calls, too many stories about places the sheriff had been warned to avoid, too many odd noises and lights at night, not to wonder.

Then, it had all died down. The strangers stopped hanging around the SurfSea, the deputies went back to patrolling wherever they wanted, kids still drank and bragged. And nobody knew whether anything had changed.

And, now, that same New Broom sheriff Thaddeus had complained about, the same New Broom who wouldn't defend the SurfSea Tavern from the tobacco Nazis even when he was on the payroll, was telling the Elks there might be another drug ring right under their noses, so keep a lookout. Which is just what the owner of Abby's storage locker had been doing when he used his spare key to break into her own, private four-and-a-half-ton stash.

Abby was lucky she wasn't waiting out her trial date in federal prison. Given the size of the haul, you would have thought she was on the DEA's ten-most-wanted list. But the Feds never got a chance at her because Siletz County got her first, and the county didn't hold her in jail. Here she was, the biggest drug bust in living memory, and the judge just looked at her during the arraignment hearing, announced she wasn't a risk for flight, and let her loose on her own recognizance. The DA didn't even object. Since then, I've wondered whether the DA might have set that up, whether he let her spend a night in jail so she would be good and scared, then had a private word with the judge to set her free to see which way she jumped. Unfortunately for whatever he hoped to find out, she jumped my way. Or, at least, I was the one she called.

There were no twelve-foot statues of Blind Justice outside the Siletz County Courthouse when I arrived to pick up Abby, and no pompous quotes carved into the pediment. Instead, the place looked like what it was, a junior high school that had been abandoned after the failure of a school-bond referendum.

A pair of public-school steel doors with panic bars opened onto wide stairs leading to a landing with a kids' mural of Sacagawea pointing out the Pacific Ocean to Lewis and Clark. Halls ran off in both directions. The ceilings were asbestos tile, and the floors were worn, institutional linoleum.

The district courtroom seemed to be in the cafeteria, and the circuit courtroom was in what looked like the auditorium. The rest of the first floor was the assessor's office. Upstairs, it was all sheriff's department and one criminal courtroom in what must have started life as a science lab. Most of the time, the three courtrooms were dark and the doors were closed—which says a lot about the people in Siletz County. That morning, they had opened up the science lab for Abby's arraignment.

The fact was, I wasn't at all sure I was ready to play in her league. Four and a half tons of marijuana wasn't some little get-your-feet-wet starter drug-defense. It was major narco-trafficking, and I knew what happened to lawyers who let major narco-traffickers go to jail.

I wasn't going to be up against a trainee district attorney in front of a senile probate judge this time. And, as for that glass-eye trick, there was no way Abby was going to pull that off again. Then there was the whole question of witnesses. We didn't even have Shelley this time. This time, the witnesses were going to be the landlord and Sheriff New Broom, and they were going to be witnessing on the wrong side.

The storage unit turned out to be . . . well, I had never seen a storage unit like that one, before. It was not one of the cheerful, orange affairs you glimpse alongside the highway. It was made of concrete block with corrugated roofing and was so overgrown with moss it looked rounded at the corners. Part of that was location. Anything that sits still for more than about fifteen minutes on the Oregon Coast is just naturally going to turn green and shaggy. But I didn't see how even a storage unit in Frenchman's Cove could grow that much moss quickly. With that much moss, we were in the presence of the great-granddaddy of the entire storage-unit industry.

The funny thing was, it didn't look all that different inside. The dope may have been in squared-off, individual bales when Abby had put it there, but you couldn't prove that from the eight-by-ten glossies the sheriff gave us. When we went through those pictures a couple of days later, the bales were such a fallen-apart, slumped-over mess they looked more like the ruins of some ancient ziggurat than anything you could smoke.

But, Abby had loved her stash, and going through those photographs set her off about the unfairness of it all. "No way there were four and a half tons," she whined. "There couldn't have been more than a ton and a half in there." She looked desperately at the pictures, as if they could save her. "Tops."

I was going to have to check, but I couldn't see how three tons, one way or the other, made much difference to the case. Either way, Abby Birdsong was the drug queenpin of Siletz County.

"Susie B. wouldn't hold anywhere near four and a half tons." Abby looked despondent. "Tell him, Shelley." Susie B. Anthony was what Abby called her truck.

Shelley hadn't been listening. "They know she wasn't selling this shit." He stabbed his finger at a photograph. "If her shit was any good, you think they'd ever let us have these pictures?"

That was a new one on me. I'd had no idea the quality of the dope had anything to do with whether the sheriff let you have pictures of it. "Come on." Shelley rattled the photograph. "If her shit was any good, the deputies wouldn't have found four and a half tons, they would have found four and a half kilos."

I must have seemed a little slow, because he modulated his voice the way sophisticated people sometimes do and told me how "the rest of it wouldn't be in the picture. It would be in a county pickup on the way to market. And, who's going to say different? You? You ready to complain to some judge that Abby actually had more dope than the sheriff busted her with?"

But, I thought, if it had only been a ton and a half, "Why jack it up to four and a half tons?"

"To get into *Sheriff's Monthly*. Biggest previous bust in Siletz County was three tons. Thing is," Shelley mused, "that probably wasn't really three, either." Behind him, Abby began crying softly.

"So." I turned to Abby, not really wanting to pick on her while she was feeling low about her stash. "Where did you get a truckload of dope in the first place?" And the story began to come out.

As it happened, there had been something to the rumors about drug drops in the early seventies. She and Shelley had just missed seeing one. They had been in Susie B. up at Neahkahnie Beach about two in the morning, when they heard gunshots. I didn't have any trouble imagining what they were doing in her truck when the shooting interrupted them.

Shelley had been a deputy sheriff, of all things, back then. He was off duty, but when they heard the shots, he and Abby ran down onto the beach to see what was up, and right there in the dunes, not fifty yards from Susie B., was a huge wall of marijuana all stacked up in bales.

Abby and Shelley hid in the dune grass for a long time, but whoever had been doing the shooting and, for that matter, whoever had been doing the getting shot at, had run off, and it was just Abby and Shelley and Susie B. and a wall of marijuana. After a while, they worked up enough nerve to do the obvious thing.

Susie B. was a big, American pickup, and she held a lot of dope. Too much, really. Nobody can smoke a ton and a half of anything in one lifetime. But, knowing she had a ton and a half in a storage unit, well, it gave Abby a sense of confidence about the future. No matter what else happened, Abby Birdsong wouldn't have to worry about where her next toke was coming from.

23

SIX O'CLOCK in the morning, the Saturday after Abby was busted, deputies showed up at my house with a warrant to search for the ancient Spanish treasure I had hidden around the place. The Department of Justice had made its move.

Actually, the deputies showed up a few strokes before six, but close enough to call it six if I tried to make something of it. The rules only let them execute search warrants in "daylight hours," but long before I'd come on the scene, some wag in the judiciary had interpreted daylight hours to mean any time between six in the morning and ten at night. So, when the sheriff wants to intimidate you, he shows up a few strokes before six and starts your Saturday off with a bang. It's Saturday because that way, if he finds anything, he gets to hold you in jail until a judge shows up on Monday and lets you go.

Everything seemed to be pretty much in order. The warrant looked like a warrant. Something that could have been the signature of a judge was on the bottom. My name was spelled correctly, the address was my address, and there wasn't any ambiguity about what the deputies were looking for:

1. All ancient treasures of Spanish or Oriental origin to include all objects of gold, silver, or other precious metals, or of porcelain or ivory, to include specie, religious or ecclesiastical ware, loose gems, or proceeds thereof, taken from State of Oregon land on Neahkahnie Mountain, or from beneath Neahkahnie Beach, or from State waters off Neahkahnie Beach, or off Neahkahnie Mountain, or from adjoining beaches or waters;

How, exactly, the deputies were supposed to identify where the ancient treasure had been taken from wasn't spelled out. And it wasn't just treasure they were looking for. They wanted everything I had on Engine Joe, too.

2. all documents and other physical material relating to, or in any way tending to identify, one Engine Joe, believed to be a resident of Siletz County or Tillamook County, Oregon . . .

Faced with a warrant I had no basis for objecting to, I did the only thing I could do. I told the deputies I objected. By then, I knew a lot more about search warrants than I had when the police had tossed Thaddeus's office.

That I objected wasn't going to keep anybody out of my house. I was just a lawyer, after all, and they had guns. If I objected too loudly, they'd arrest me for interfering with a legally authorized search. The thing that made this different from Stalinist Russia was that if I objected and it turned out something really was wrong with the warrant, I got to complain about it later. But, only if I'd objected.

The objection taken care of, I went to dance step number two of the Kabuki Dance of the Search Warrant and demanded to see the affidavit setting out the facts the warrant was based on.

That stopped them for a while. I don't think they were used to people demanding to see the affidavit, and the deputy in charge went back to his car and had a little conference on the radio with somebody about it. While he was out there, I skipped directly to dance step number four and went inside and called Lydia Stonemason to come save me. She didn't sound as surprised as I had been to be awakened at six on a Saturday morning, and she said she would be right over.

Then I returned to the porch and back to dance step number three, which I had skipped, and asked one of the assistant deputies to please delay the search until my lawyer arrived. Strictly speaking, I should have asked the deputy in charge, but he was still in the patrol car, consulting with his radio on what to do about the affidavit. The sheriff's department must have had to wake up its own lawyer, because it was a while before he came back.

When he did, he informed me that, one, there wasn't any requirement they show me any affidavit, and, two, even if there were, he wasn't going to show me this particular affidavit because the judge had put it under seal, and, three, since I was a lawyer, myself, there wasn't any point in waiting for any more cocksucking lawyers to show up.

I pointed out that it didn't make any difference what I did for a living, I was entitled to have my lawyer present.

He pointed back out that I was welcome to pay whomever I wanted to come watch his men search my house, but, since my lawyer couldn't do anything to stop them from searching, they were going to get started right now. And, meanwhile, I would be sitting here on the porch where I would be out of the way.

I pointed out that my only obligation was not to interfere with the search, and since it was my house, I would be inside taking movies of his deputies while they went through my things.

He pointed out that the minute I switched on a motherfucking movie camera, I would be interfering with their search, and he would personally run me down to the county jail.

I went into the dining room where I had been dictating some documents for Grady and came back with a handheld cassette recorder, switched it on, and pointed out all over again that since it was my house, I would be taking movies while his people conducted their search.

He pointed out to the cassette recorder that I was welcome to take all the movies I wanted but, please, do not interfere with any deputies during the execution of the duly-signed-and-legal search warrant the law required them to execute at my house.

I pointed out that there was no way that merely taking movies could possibly interfere with anybody's deputyly duties. Then I stepped out to the driveway and retrieved Abby's movie camera from the trunk of my car where I had been holding it for her since the county had returned it after the trial. When I tried to get back in the house, some-body had locked the door and I didn't have a key in the pocket of my bathrobe.

I did have a key in the downspout, but by the time I got inside and began filming, the kitchen drawers were already dumped onto the floor. The deputy in charge looked into the camera, shrugged a what-can-you-do? kind of shrug, and pointed out what a lousy housekeeper I was.

Outside, Lydia Stonemason screeched up in a butter-colored, beau-tifully restored, 1959 Karmann Ghia. When she'd said she'd be right over, she meant she'd be right over just as soon as she could get her clothes on and into her car and figure out the quickest route to where I lived. All in all, it didn't take that long.

She strode inside, looking even taller and more angular than usual, and a lot scarier than I ever managed. Part of that was profession-alism, but part of it was from having been woken up sooner than she wanted, and having less time than she needed to get herself together. She didn't seem happy about any of it. "Sam," she said when she saw the deputy in charge. "What the hell is going on in here?"

"Executing a search warrant." Sam gestured at me. "This your client?" The way he said *this* didn't make me feel as though he thought she should be proud to have my business.

"Damn straight he's my client," Lydia said, sounding honored to be my lawyer. It was a nice touch.

"Well, he's being a real smart-ass and—"

"Looks to me"—she glanced at the mess on the kitchen floor—"he has call to be a lot more than just a smart-ass." Then she asked for Sam's card. That way, there wouldn't be any doubt who had been in charge of this shambles.

Damn, I thought. Why didn't I think of that?

When she went around and asked the other deputies for their cards, it turned out it wasn't just Sam who knew her. They all did, and as soon as they heard her voice, the search became a lot less noisy and a lot more orderly.

"They going to find anything?" she whispered when she returned to where I was standing.

"Spanish treasure?" I laughed. "You kidding?"

Then she asked an odd question. "Is the affidavit under seal?"

I nodded.

"Thought so." She gestured toward a couple of assistant deputies rummaging through the stack of files I had been working on in the dining room. "Get this on film," she whispered. Then she turned to the deputies.

"Those papers you are so casually pawing through are legal files. They are protected by the attorney-client privilege. They are also protected as work product and for half a dozen other reasons I am not going to go into right now. I would highly suggest that you put them down immediately." The assistant deputies dropped the files as quickly as if their wives had caught them going through love letters from old girlfriends. "The fact that you have examined them may already have irredeemably tainted your case," Lydia said in a cold voice.

"I doubt it," Sam said from behind us.

He walked into the dining room and picked up one of the files and looked at the name. Then dropped it onto the table with a flat little smack and picked up a couple of others. He checked those names, too. "These may actually be legal files, for all I know," he said. "But they are for some guy named Grady Jackson, and since Mr. Jackson is not the subject of this investigation, we haven't tainted a damn thing."

"Maybe," Lydia said back. "But if it turns out that the investigation of Grady Jackson is coordinated with this investigation, you may have tainted both cases."

Sam had a great poker face, but it didn't take a card player to notice that he put down the files and walked out of the dining room, and that nobody from the sheriff's department ever touched any of Grady's files again.

After a long time, the deputies ran out of places to rummage through and wrapped up their treasure hunt and left. And I had won. They hadn't found any ancient treasure. They hadn't found any secret documents revealing the true identity of Engine Joe. And they hadn't found anything else to use against me.

I thanked Lydia, and she left, too. I was just starting to pick up the mess in the kitchen when Grady called, and I had to hightail it over to the Coast.

Whatever had made Lydia suspect the cases were coordinated, she had been right. At a few minutes before six, state troopers had shown up with a warrant to search Grady's house. And, they had found something.

24

WHAT THEY HAD found was Grady's beautiful gold chain. The warrant was identical to the one the Multnomah County deputies had served me:

> All ancient treasures of Spanish or Oriental origin to include all objects of gold, silver, or other precious metals, or of porcelain or ivory, to include specie, religious or ecclesiastical ware, loose gems, or proceeds thereof blah blah blah . . .

They had written it that way, Lydia told me later, so Grady and I would know that it wasn't just a coincidence, that the DOJ was calling the shots.

"They gave me a ticket for it, a by-God ticket." Grady glared at the mess the troopers had made of his living room. "Here." He shoved a balled-up wad of paper into my hand.

It was a ticket, all right: a citation to appear in court in ten days on the charge of being in possession of stolen property. Specifically:

Heavy Gold Chain, of Spanish or Oriental Origin (1 ea)

"Here I've got a court order that won't let me come anywhere closer than a hundred yards to the beach, not even for a picnic, and they confiscate my chain from me because I'm supposed to of dug it up on the beach." Grady's face was the reddest I had ever seen it. "If they really thought I stole the chain, I should be in jail."

"You'll get your chance," I told him quietly. "They don't want to tip their hand."

"Tip their hand? They want to keep my chain."

"They want to keep you." I'd had a lot of time to think this through on the drive over.

If they arrested him, the DA would have to convince a judge he had probable cause to believe Grady had committed a crime. That meant a formal hearing, and a hearing meant I would get the chance to cross-examine the DA's witnesses and learn a lot more about his case than he wanted me to know just then.

The way to avoid all that was to write Grady a ticket. While he was waiting to appear in court, the DA could call together a grand jury, tell the grand jurors Grady had been caught with a stolen chain, and get them to issue an indictment. Then, when Grady showed up about the ticket, the sheriff could arrest him on the spot, without anybody ever having to show the judge—or me—anything.

"So what I need to do," Grady said, "is go down and explain to that grand jury how I couldn't possibly of stolen the chain from state land because I'm not even allowed on state land and—"

"Can't do it," I told him. "The DA is the only one who gets to present evidence to a grand jury. If he doesn't call you, you don't get to tell them anything."

"You mean"—for a crazy guy, Grady was pretty quick on the uptake—"the DA can go in there, tell a bunch of lies, and get me indicted, and I don't get to tell my side of the story?"

"Telling your side of the story is what the trial's for."

"I don't want to go to trial. That's the whole point. Can't you stop this before there's a trial?"

"Not if the district attorney wants you indicted."

"Then I need to have a talk with Mr. District Attorney."

That was really a bad idea. Nobody ever helps his case by explaining to a district attorney why the charges should be dropped. The district attorney is not interested in dropping charges. The district attorney is interested in hearing what you have to say so he can use it against you. But bad idea or not, there was no way I was going to talk Grady Jackson out of going down to the DA's office.

25

W E MET WITH the DA in a threadbare little conference room on the second floor of the Siletz County Courthouse, in what had probably been a storage closet before the school-bond initiative failed.

Some dormant survival instinct must have kicked in, because Grady had shaved that morning. His hair was trimmed and neatly combed. He had on a tidy hunting jacket and clean khakis. And he didn't say anything about the cornerstones from King Solomon's temple, or the Mystical Name of Great Power, or scrolls with hidden information about the future, or chambers carved beneath Neahkahnie Mountain, or jailbird monks, or Spanish treasure ships mentioned in the Bible. All together, Grady went into the DA's office at his sanest and most convincing. But it didn't last. By the time he came out, he had told the DA, and the DA's tape recorder, that he'd gotten the chain on a secret mission to the king of Arabia.

Grady began, rationally enough, by handing the DA a copy of the court order barring him from Neahkahnie Beach. The DA glanced at the order and jotted something on a yellow pad, then asked Grady why the court order had been issued.

"For diggin' at night."

"Digging at night." The DA nodded and wrote something else on his pad. He was a tall, sorrowful-looking guy who had made a career out of being skeptical, and he did not give the impression he was going to make an exception in Grady's case.

"Yes, sir," Grady agreed in his crispest, most military manner. "The neighbors claimed I'd been runnin' a backhoe . . ." The district attorney raised his hand for silence, and Grady proved just how serious he was about being sane by actually shutting up.

"So, you're telling me I should drop the charges," the DA said in a puzzled voice, "because the only way you could have stolen that chain was by digging on a state beach where you aren't allowed to dig, which is the very thing you got thrown off the same state beach for doing in the first place? Is that it?" The DA waited long enough for the ridiculousness of Grady's logic to sink in, then did what he had been planning to do since I'd called to set up the meeting. He hijacked the discussion.

He started by sliding a photograph across the table to Grady. "You know what these markings are?" It was a blowup of one of the links of Grady's chain. The link was engraved in an elegant, curved script.

"Arabic," Grady said. "Looks like Arabic."

"It's Arabic, alright, but it's not modern." The DA took the photo back. "It's a medieval Arabic script called Kufic. That chain is old. And the writing is from the Koran. We had it translated. All the links have verses from the Koran in Kufic." The DA gave Grady a mournful look. "This is the kind of thing you'd expect to find on a Spanish ship wrecked on the Oregon Coast three or four hundred years ago, wouldn't you say?" He folded his hands, waiting for Grady to say.

Grady was still sane enough not to say and just kept examining the photograph as if he thought he could spot something the DA had missed. After a while, the DA got tired of waiting and changed the subject.

"You grew up in Kentucky?"

"Flat Lick." Grady nodded.

The DA jotted another note. "Since then, you've lived on the Coast?"

"Except when I was in the army."

"You ran that bar in Frenchman's Cove?"

"SurfSea. It's called the SurfSea."

"Shoot a man in there?"

That came out of the blue. There was no way Grady was going to be charged with that shooting. Not now. We all knew that. But it was disconcerting the district attorney brought it up.

"He was tryin' to take advantage of my regulars," Grady started to explain, as if shooting a man were just one of the services he provided his customers. "He was sellin' shares in a string of mules to go up the Pearl River in Red China and come back with a load of cheap silver—"

"You shot a man for claiming he had a string of mules?" The DA was at his most astonished.

"Not because of the mules." Grady was beginning to look a little uncomfortable. "He was swindling money from my customers to—"

"But you did shoot him?" The DA looked even more sorrowful than before, as if realizing all over again what a wicked, wicked world we live in.

Grady nodded.

"Now what I want to know is"—the DA switched the conversation again—"what a good country boy like you who's never been out of the United States was doing with something so . . . unusual . . . as that chain if you didn't dig it up." He was good at keeping people off-balance.

"I did some travelin' in the army," Grady said, not exactly answering the question.

"That chain come from Guadalcanal?" the DA asked, making Grady sound silly all over again.

"I stayed in after the war." Grady's words began to speed up as he slipped into the land of the completely insane and began telling how the chain was a gift from the king of Arabia.

"You are telling me"—the DA fiddled with a knob on the tape recorder to make sure he didn't lose a word Grady was saying—"that you know the king of Arabia?"

"Not just me. There were five of us." Grady leaned toward the DA and lowered his voice almost to a whisper, as if he were revealing a secret. "We were on a mission."

"And all five of you on that mission"—the DA was at his most skeptical—"came away with medieval gold chains?"

"No." Grady looked surprised at the question. "The others got other things. The chain was a sign for me. A sign . . ." Grady glanced at the door to make sure nobody was eavesdropping. "They had jeweled boxes in there, and golden goblets, and saddles sewn all over with pearls, and sword belts going back to the time of the Prophet, and loose gems. All the treasures of Ali Baba, and you could just gather up whatever you wanted. But nobody besides me got that chain, so you tell me that doesn't mean something . . ." Grady ground to a halt, as if he suspected he might have given away too much.

"You got paperwork?" the DA asked. "Something you can show that traces that chain back to—"

"Paperwork," Grady snorted. "It ain't like I got a bill of sale from the king of Arabia. Then I had to sneak it past my own goddamn government so, no, I don't exactly have any written paperwork."

"Pictures, maybe. A photograph of you and the king?"

"King Abdul Aziz ibn Saud would never show off like that," Grady said quietly, as if the DA didn't know the first thing about Arabian etiquette.

"How about witnesses? Anybody besides you see—"

"My sister."

"Your sister?" the DA asked, as if the very existence of a sister were a new one on him.

"Ellie." Grady's face was starting to turn red. He was used to people pretending to believe him. "I spend January and February with her in Tucson."

"Oh?" The DA wrote a note to himself. "Your sister in Arizona . . . was with you on a secret mission when the king of Arabia gave you the chain? That was in nineteen . . ."

"Fifty-one. I got the chain in 1951. It took me twenty years to understand what it meant."

"Your sister will testify she was in Arabia in 1951 when King Abdool . . ."

"Abdul Aziz," Grady corrected him. "King Abdul Aziz ibn Saud."

". . . King Abdool Aziz gave you that chain?"

"My sister will testify that she saw the chain when I came home in 1951," Grady said, and skipped back into the land of the sane as easily as if the border were made of soap bubbles. "And if you think you are going to charge me with stealing something thirty years ago, you better do some serious checking into the statute of limitations."

"Yeah," I chimed in, as if I had thought of it on my own.

"Well, you just get that sister of yours to come tell the jury you had that chain thirty years ago, and we'll see about the statute of limitations." From the way the DA said it, he seemed to know more about Ellie than Grady wanted him to know.

I guess he did, too. Every time I tried to get Grady to have her tell me what she'd seen, there was always a windstorm in Arizona and the lines were down, or she was off working the slots in Vegas, or she had forgotten to pay her bill and the phone was turned off—and Grady never seemed to follow up. The time came when I began to suspect that, whatever it was she knew, Grady didn't want her anywhere near the DA. After a while, I let it drop and began preparing his defense without her.

"You the one," the DA said, switching gears on Grady, again, "talked all that pig latin to the Japanese?" I didn't have the whole story, then, but pig latin had something to do with what Grady had done on Guadalcanal.

"*Japs,*" Grady replied with quiet dignity. "I would appreciate it if you'd refer to our recent adversaries as *Japs.*"

The DA switched off the tape recorder and turned back to Grady. "Something I think is, you are talking pig latin to me, now. Something else I think is, you dug up that chain the night you were kicked off the beach." He slid Grady's court order into a file folder. "And the third thing I think is, I can prove it."

"You can't prove squat because I own that chain fair and square."

"What I can prove"—the DA raised his hand for silence—"is that you have been living up there on Neahkahnie Mountain for what, nine years?"

"Ten." Grady glared at him.

"Ten years, and that whole time you haven't had a job and you haven't had any other income anybody can see. So—"

"It's no crime"—this time, I was the one who interrupted—"not to have a job."

"No." The DA leaned back in his chair. "But it is a crime to steal sunken treasure from state land. And, like I said, your client has been living off something all these years."

"It's no goddamn business of yours"—Grady shoved his huge, flat face across the table at the DA—"or any goddamn body else's, what I live off of."

"Maybe." For such a sorrowful guy, the DA seemed to be enjoying himself an awful lot. "But you have been living off something. There's no getting around that. And the jury is liable to make assumptions about what. And, if you haven't been living off stolen treasure like I think, then you still haven't had any income and you sure weren't spending income you didn't have to buy something as fancy as that chain. So, unless you can show how you come by it legitimately, you stole it, just like I said."

That was bullshit, and the DA knew it. By making Grady show he was the rightful owner of his own chain, he was making the defendant prove his innocence. The problem was, it was the kind of bullshit that might stick. Things would have been simpler if Grady had just stayed home—which fact Lydia Stonemason pointed out to me two days later.

26

SHE'D WANTED TO get to the bottom of why the searches of my house and Grady's had been coordinated, so she'd talked to some people she knew. When she had it figured out, she called and asked whether I drank Scotch. That was as good a way as any to work up to the scary news she had to deliver.

I told her I liked Scotch a lot better than the bourbon everybody else involved with Grady's case seemed to drink.

"It's a good thing," she told me. "You are about to make the acquaintance of the Siletz County judge. He doesn't stand on a lot of formality, and Scotch is part of the deal. Usually he invites both sides into chambers and discusses the case. Then, when he's figured out how he's going to rule, he steps into the courtroom and puts it into the record. You've already met the district attorney over there."

"Sorrowful kind of guy, if you ask me."

"Don't let that fool you. I've worked with him a few times, and he's as ambitious as they come. His problem is, there isn't much for a district attorney to be ambitious about in Siletz County. Just that one judge he has to kiss up to every day. I'm not saying anything out of school, here. Everybody knows that.

"What everybody is not supposed to know is that a career opportunity has opened up at the Department of Justice for a candidate with the right experience. And the department just happened to think of the DA in Siletz County, and what a good job he's been doing all these years prosecuting criminals. Just one loose end needs to be taken care of, first. Before the DOJ passes out any new jobs, it wants him to find out where the treasure that keeps showing up on the market is coming from. But that's no big deal. The DOJ can even give him some help with it. It seems they've traced the stolen treasure to the crooked lawyer in Portland who fenced it." She paused a minute to see how I would take that.

I cleared my throat, but there wasn't really much to say. Then she picked back up. "Even though the crooked lawyer has moved on to that big cellblock in the sky, the DOJ still had some thoughts about where some of the treasure might have wound up and arranged to have a couple of likely houses searched. Well, they didn't find the mother lode, but the state troopers did turn up one very old, very gold chain. Which would have been more than enough to scare any ordinary person into playing ball and turning over the rest of the treasure. But, wouldn't you know it, the person they caught with the chain isn't your ordinary guy. He's a crazy old recluse who hasn't played ball with anybody since he refused to make up his bed in the army. So, the DOJ thought, maybe the trick is to convince the crazy old recluse's lawyer to get him to hand over the treasure.

"As luck would have it, the lawyer in question used to work for the very same crooked attorney who'd been fencing the treasure in the first place, which gives the DA some leverage. Now the part nobody's supposed to know, because nobody is ever supposed to know what goes on in front of a grand jury, is that the DA thinks that if he arrests the lawyer . . ."

Me? The DA wants to arrest ME?

". . . the crazy old recluse will find himself under a lot of pressure to turn over the treasure, and as part of the deal, the lawyer can turn over whatever bagatelles may have fallen into his hands, as well. So, now, the DA's asking the grand jury for a pair of indictments, one against Grady for stealing the treasure. The other against you for conspiring to fence it."

"I never fenced anything," I think I was starting to sputter. "And if Thaddeus was fencing something, I didn't know about it. I didn't have any idea what was going on in his office. I just thought he was hiding from his sister."

"Doesn't make any difference. The DA knows what Thaddeus was doing in his office. And, now that he's not in his office any longer, the DA's going after you. The part you have to remember"—Lydia sounded almost cheerful—"is that, ambitious as that DA is, this isn't an easy one for him. Before he can convict anybody, he's got to prove Grady violated the Sunken Treasure Act, and all he's got to work with is that one gold chain. If the troopers had caught Grady with a whole chest of buried treasure, that would be different. But a single gold chain could have come from anywhere. All Grady needs is one believable reason why he owns the chain, and both of you are off the hook. Surely he can come up with something, don't you think?"

There, without actually advising me to have Grady lie, Lydia had told me exactly how he had to testify. Unfortunately, a believable reason was the one thing he was not going to be able to come up with, now that he was on record with that king-of-Arabia bullshit.

27

THE MORNING GRADY reported to court on his citation for stealing the chain, there weren't any surprises. The grand jury had passed out an indictment, just as the DA had wanted, the county opened up the science lab just for him, the sheriff had the warrant, and Grady was arrested on the spot. I was worried the sheriff would have a warrant for me, too, but he didn't. Instead, the judge, the DA, and I retired to chambers to sip whiskey and argue about it. Grady had to wait out in the courtroom under the watchful eye of the sheriff.

I liked that old judge. He kept his robe on a hook, he wasn't wearing a tie, and he poured each of us a Scotch before we sat down. He had a full-size American flag next to the window, an enormous, standing grizzly bear carved out of a single cedar log in the corner, and a blue-and-white golf umbrella on a gun rack, but no guns. He kept a well-thumbed set of the *Oregon Revised Statutes* on the shelf behind his desk, but he didn't seem to have any books of case law. I got the impression he wasn't interested in what other judges thought.

"My first big client was a chain-saw artist," he explained when he noticed me looking at the bear. "He didn't have much cash to pay me with." Then he turned to the DA and told him almost exactly the same thing Lydia had told me. "I'd be a lot happier if you had a chest filled with buried treasure. One gold chain isn't a lot to go on if you want to convict somebody under the Sunken Treasure Act. Anybody can own a gold chain. In fact"—he smiled at the DA—"I have a pair of gold chains, myself." I couldn't have said it better.

The DA pointed out that Grady had already been found guilty of illegally digging for buried treasure on Neahkahnie Beach, then he handed the judge a copy of Grady's restraining order. It was the same restraining order Grady had given him a few days earlier to prove he couldn't have dug up the chain on the beach.

Next, the DA tried to make a big deal out of the engraved verses from the Koran. He told us he'd found somebody at the Tillamook County Pioneer Museum who would testify the verses proved Grady had stolen the chain from public land.

The judge didn't buy any of it, and, I think, he was on the verge of dismissing the charges right then. But the DA pointed out that this was an arraignment hearing, and that the grand jury had already decided there was enough evidence to go forward. The DA looked even more sorrowful than usual, as if it pained him to have to explain something so simple to a judge.

"Very well," the old judge told him, "I don't have any choice but to set a trial date, but I hope you know what you're doing. If that gold chain is the only evidence of sunken treasure you've got, you better be sure it's solid, or I'm going to look very favorably on a motion for a judgment of acquittal when the time comes." I liked that judge.

"It's solid gold," the DA joked.

"See that it is," the judge told him, not sounding amused.

"It's good as gold," the DA said, trying to make the same joke, again, as if the judge hadn't gotten it the first time. Then he asked that bail be set at $500,000.

That was outrageous, and I said so. Here my client was charged, essentially, with the crime of being too poor to own something as nice as that chain, and the DA was asking for bail that a rich person would have had trouble coming up with. Then I pointed out that this same court, meaning he, this same judge, had recently agreed with this same DA to let the largest accused marijuana dealer in county history, meaning Abby Birdsong, go home and wait for trial with no bail at all.

The judge must have thought there was something to that, because he set bail at $50. "What's a few zeros among friends?" He grinned at the DA. I got the impression that they weren't fond of each other.

Then the judge stood and led us back into the courtroom to put what he had decided into the record.

When I sat down next to Grady, he fished in the pocket of his best, going-to-court hunting jacket. "Five grand," he whispered, and slipped me a roll of twenties beneath the counsel table. "Run these down to the bank and get a cashier's check. Use the rest to pay yourself what I owe you." I wasn't sure why he didn't just hand over the money to the court, but I did as I was told. Judging by the bulges in the ammo pockets, I think he had been prepared to go a good deal higher than $50.

There was a line at the bank. Then, when it was my turn, the teller got embroiled in a phone conversation with somebody who wanted his checking-account statements mailed on the fifth of the month instead of the third. When I finally had her attention, it took her longer than it should have to count and arrange all three twenties so that each bill was right-side up and facing the same way. When she had them tallied and organized the way she wanted, she counted them twice more, just to make sure. Then she had to consult with the manager to locate the form for making out a cashier's check. After that, she had to make out the check, and check the check to make sure she had made it out properly. And then she had to rustle up a couple of witnesses to make sure that when I signed, I really signed. So it seemed like a long time before I got back to the courthouse.

It could have been longer, as far as Grady was concerned. When I walked back into the courtroom, he was sitting in the witness chair telling the sheriff and the bailiff and the DA what it had been like running a bar on the Oregon Coast twenty years ago. The judge was in chambers, sipping whiskey and listening through the open door.

"I should have had you stop for coffee," Grady chuckled as we walked back to my car. "There's no end to what them peckerwoods will sit still for." He had enjoyed making everybody wait while I went for the check.

28

O N THE WAY back to Portland, I stopped in Tillamook to check out the Pioneer Museum. I wanted to see for myself why verses from the Koran proved Grady's chain had been stolen from state land.

The museum is in an awkward, two-story building with a peaked roof that gives the impression of a prosperous home encroached upon by urbanization. On second glance, it's hard to imagine why any home would be standing alone in the middle of a block in downtown Tillamook—or how anything in Tillamook could have been encroached upon by urbanization. Or, for that matter, why a house should have a mammoth piece of sawmill equipment resting on two enormous logs in the yard.

On third glance, it doesn't look like a house—the windows are too tall, and it's not made of wood like every other home in the Pacific Northwest. It's hard to tell under the paint, but the place appears to be built of sandstone blocks. The more you stare at it, the more it looks like what it is—a discarded courthouse turned into a local museum. Inside, the rooms are such a jumble of odd sizes and disorienting connections, it's hard to get any sense of the overall layout— as if the contractor had mistaken the solution to a tangram puzzle for architectural drawings

The objects on display are as unlikely, and as unrelated, as the rooms—which is to say, the Tillamook County Pioneer Museum is a huge, glorious flea market of odds and ends of daily life over the last 150 years. An entire room is filled with military uniforms and personal equipment brought home from an assortment of wars. Another room contains elegant dolls—glass, and porcelain, and lead—from the nineteenth century. Yet another, a full-scale replica of the hollowed-out tree stump a settler named Joe Champion lived in when he moved to the county in 1851.

Upstairs in the windowless space beneath the peaked roof is a riot of taxidermy. Stuffed ducks and geese, poorly lit salmon, and woodland creatures compete in the shadows with a pronghorn, a fox, an ill-tempered-looking raccoon, a leopard, a snarling baboon, an eagle in full flight, and the heads of more elk than are painted on the walls of the most effusive prehistoric French cave. If not actually the attic of Hermann Göring's hunting lodge, this is a trophy room of which the Reichsmarschall would heartily have approved.

There's a shingle-covered cabin in the basement that used to sit on a fire tower, a mishmash of household appliances, and a full-size Smokey the Bear in a glass case looking like a stand-up version of Sleeping Beauty. Or Lenin. He is wearing blue jeans, carrying a shovel, and, naturally, sporting a Smokey the Bear hat.

In the Tillamook County Pioneer Museum, you are never far from the pioneers themselves. Black-and-white, portrait-size photographs of grim, square-bearded men and their fierce-looking women cover the walls and stairwells. Gazing into those unyielding eyes, you are left with a couple of impressions. The first is that, no matter how remote you imagine this part of the world must have been a hundred and some years ago, it certainly supported an active portrait-photography business. The other thought you are left with is, thank God Almighty I didn't commit a crime back then and wind up with these people on my jury.

The museum doesn't make a big deal out of things found near Neahkahnie Mountain, but they're there. And they are strange and suggestive and, above all, real. You can't walk through that museum and not know, for sure, that something big once happened out there.

The treasure rocks are in the basement, in a room with a 1909 Buick, a 1906 stagecoach, a horse-drawn sleigh, and a whole wall of saddles. The saddles seem to be in good repair, but the stagecoach appears saggy, and the Buick is resting on its hubs.

The treasure rocks are big and look heavy. One is potato-shaped, carved with an *E*, a *W*, a *D*, an arrow, and a row of dots, all as plain as day—and all just as strange, and as familiar, as you imagined, and as hard to make sense of as they were for the generations of people who have already tried to make sense of them.

Whatever else I might have expected, I imagined the treasure rocks among grass and sand and salt spray. Behind glass in the basement of a museum, they look diminished. But there is no arguing with their solidity. No matter what odd dreams the rocks may have inspired, they are real.

More treasure rocks are shoved in a corner underneath the wall of saddles, and impossible to get at because a huge, red, spoke-wheeled fire-hose cart is in the way. In the dim light, I could make out a feathered shaft on one, a letter carved into the other.

Five more are in the corner behind the display case—rocks I take on faith are treasure rocks, but I can't really tell. I can't identify any particular markings except one—a clearly incised, approximately fifty-degree angle. It is, I realize, the very rock that Hiram Smith found in 1869 that started all the years of treasure hunting.

Back upstairs, Sam Reed's bronze chest handles are stored away like ancient butterflies in a neat, glass-topped specimen box. I have to ask to see them. Like the other things the museum has squirreled away from public view, the handles give the impression of being better organized and better cared-for than anything on display.

Seeing the chest handles is a little like seeing the treasure rocks. They are there. They are as advertised. And I can't help feeling a little disappointed. Whatever they are, they most certainly are not the massive, brazen handles from a sixteenth-century strongbox I had imagined. They are delicate, more like drawer pulls from a lady's dresser. Or, when I think about it, the kind of elegant, Oriental chest you might store silk in. And silk is a real possibility if whatever lies wrecked off Nehalem Spit did really come from the Orient. Along with the chest handles, the museum has a handful of small shards of sixteenth-century Ming porcelain collected from Indian sites that may have come from the same wreck, but it's hard to know.

They also have one of the teakwood walking sticks Pat Smith carved out of boards he pulled from the ship sunk off Nehalem Spit. The walking stick is rough-sawn and reddish, practical but not finished or polished or, even, particularly well-sanded—showing the qualities, I like to believe, of the man who made it.

There's a silver holy-oil vessel taken from the wreck, as well. It is the kind of thing that seems as if it would come off a Catholic ship. And, if that ship was Spanish, as Pat Smith thought, what sank with it may be very valuable indeed.

Something that almost certainly proves Spaniards were here is a large block of old beeswax. Beeswax has been on Nehalem Spit for a long time. Lewis and Clark mentioned it in their journals. But it's older than that. The chunk in the Pioneer Museum has been carbon-dated to between 1500 and 1650.

Beeswax does not deteriorate in weather, and the first settlers found between twelve and twenty tons stacked on Nehalem Spit. Some of the chunks were marked with symbols of the Catholic Church. Some had a cross and a circle. Some were marked with Roman numerals, others, Arabic.

Most of the beeswax was shipped to Hawaii, where, as in early North America, there were no European honeybees to make candles. When the price of wax reached twenty cents a pound in Astoria, an enterprising prospector staked a beeswax claim and extracted three more tons, making, when you think about what that twenty cents is worth in current dollars, beeswax mining the only enterprise known to have made a profit from anything found around Neahkahnie Mountain.

In the glass case, the beeswax looks hard, ivory-colored, and dully shiny, like a block of carved soapstone or enameled wood. And, it's big. Maybe a foot by fifteen inches by a foot. A large *67* is indented on the face, with part of what may be a *1* broken off on the left, and a fragment of what seems to be a *9* to the right that, together, suggest the number 1679. Which, in its turn, may be a date that has something to do with the time the ship sailed. Or, perhaps, an inventory number of some sort.

Pollen taken from the wax is from a species of holly that grows in northern Luzon in the Philippines. It's that connection with the Philippines—and with the Orient and the Catholic Church and Araby—that makes a lot of people think the ship buried off Nehalem Spit is a Manila galleon.

29

THE MANILA GALLEONS were the biggest ships Spain made. In the sixteenth century, before the merchants back in Seville lobbied the king to limit their size, Manila galleons averaged between 1,700 and 2,000 tons, fully loaded. Afterward, they weren't supposed to be any bigger than 300 tons, but the shipyards in Cavite were a long way from Seville, and galleons of 700, 1,000, and even 2,000 tons frequent the records.

They were not meant to be fast. Spain controlled the entrances to the Pacific at Cape Horn and Panama and claimed title to the entire ocean as a mare nostrum. They did not expect to have to outrun enemies on those waters and, for the most part, never met any. The galleons were meant to be big and sturdy and capable of hauling enormous loads planetary distances. They were partially constructed of teak cut on Luzon. The planking was made of lanang wood, which was strong enough to repel cannon shot. The sails were woven in the Philippines, and Manila hemp made some of the finest rigging in the world.

By rule of thumb, the proportions of a galleon were 3:2:1: the length of the keel was three times the width of the ship. And the width was twice the depth of the hold. Galleons were tubby, plodding vessels by any standards, and the men who sailed them called them flying pigs.

In 1493, Pope Alexander VI drew a line around the world to keep the Spaniards and the Portuguese out of each other's hair. The Philippines were in Spanish waters—but the Spaniards could only get there by sailing west from America. This explains the odd facts that the islands were administered by the viceroy of Mexico, all communications were conducted across the Pacific to Acapulco, and the Church in Manila was part of the Diocese of Mexico City.

Lengthy as the trip from Acapulco to Manila was, it was much easier than getting back to Mexico. All a captain had to do to get to the Philippines was head south, pick up the stable and predictable trade winds, and ride the breezes. The return trip was so dangerous and so hard to navigate that, even though Magellan made it to the Philippines in 1521, no Spaniard ever returned to Mexico until 1565, when Miguel López de Legazpi worked his way north along the coast of Japan, picked up the westerlies, rode a series of storm fronts across the top of the Pacific to North America, and then made his way south along the coast to Mexico.

Once the route was established, the Pacific circuit became the longest, most remote, and one of the most dangerous and lucrative regularly scheduled commercial voyages in history—not because the Philippines produced anything particularly interesting to the Spanish, but because Manila was the major European trading port for that part of the Orient.

The Manila trade was so valuable to the Chinese that they created an entire industry manufacturing rosaries and reliquaries, vestments, crucifixes, and other Christian devotional objects for sale to priests and cathedrals throughout Latin America. Profane goods turned out to be just as profitable, and China's finest jewelers turned out rings, pendants, earrings, precious metals set with gemstones, fans, combs, mantillas, buckles, daggers, jewel-encrusted sword hilts, flasks, snuff-boxes, and all the other luxury goods a well-appointed conquistador, or his doña, might fancy. But it wasn't just the Chinese who were in on the action. Merchants and craftsmen came from all over the Eastern world to do business in Manila.

Every July, for 250 years, a galleon, sometimes two, loaded with a high-end cargo of jade; mercury; civet for perfume; damasks, ornate silverware and worked gold from Araby; taffetas, bolts of silk, inlaid woods, lacquered boxes, porcelain, and jewelry from Cathay; rugs, tapestries, woolens, and bedcoverings from Persia and Greater India; ivory and balsam from Kampuchea; sapphires, topazes, and rubies from Lesser India and Serendib; diamonds from Goa; camphor from Borneo; cloves, nutmeg, and allspice from the Moluccas; amber; beeswax; beautiful Oriental slave girls; and black Nubian eunuchs in turbans would set out from Manila Bay, head for Guam, then north to the waters off Japan, to start across the Pacific. And that was just what appeared on the manifests—when there were manifests.

Manifests let the authorities in Mexico know what to tax. When the merchants could arrange it, the galleons sailed without them. Even with manifests, something like half of the cargoes were contraband and not registered at all. In fact, smuggling was the only thing that made the trip worthwhile for the crew. Wages were so low that a captain who did not allow his sailors to smuggle could wind up with his entire crew jumping ship at the first landfall.

In fact, captains were the biggest players. In an age of payola and kickbacks, the governor of Manila sold the captaincies for about 5 percent of what the captain could earn from his own contraband added to the gratuities and percentages he could extort from the other smugglers. But the corruption that made the system work could lead to disaster. Given the profits, the temptation to overload the ships was enormous. The *Santa Maria Magdalena* left Cavite so heavy she capsized and sank within sight of the docks.

When frightened passengers pled with Captain Ignacio Martinez to lighten ship before setting out in the *Pilar,* he replied, "To Acapulco or to purgatory." Purgatory turned out to be a reef off Guam.

In 1638, the *Nuestra Señora de la Concepción* found its own reef and sank off the southern tip of Saipan when the officers mutinied and then couldn't decide who was in charge. They mutinied because Captain Don Juan Francisco was of "little age or experience in military or naval matters." Don Juan was, "at most, twenty-two or twenty-four." He'd been given the job because the governor of Manila had loaded the ship with the gold and jewelry he took in as bribes and needed a family member in charge to keep it safe.

Every February, the population of Acapulco doubled as merchants from Mexico, Panama, Peru, and the rest of Spanish America arrived to bid on goods brought in by the galleon—most of which wound up being carried overland to Veracruz, then shipped to Havana to sail with the treasure fleet to Spain.

Heading back to Manila a few weeks after the Acapulco Fair, the galleons carried Spaniards, soldiers, priests, and between three and four million silver pesos from the mines of Taxco and Zacatecas and, sometimes, from Potosí in Upper Peru, to pay for the goods. They also carried the yearly cash subsidy from the Crown to support the government of the Philippine colony.

They would have been better off leaving the priests at home. But sixteenth- and seventeenth-century Spaniards couldn't help meddling with other people's religions, and the priests became such an affliction in Japan that, in 1638, the shogunate closed down the whole country to outsiders. Until Matthew Perry showed up in the 1850s behind the guns of the United States navy, it was worth the life of a sailor to be shipwrecked in Japan, which made the journey up the Japanese coast looking for the westerlies that much more exciting.

Even on good trips, galleons heading to Acapulco spent five months without touching land in a voyage that stretched the limits of the technology of the day. Often, the trip was much longer. For the people on board, it was endless weeks of living with lice and fleas in sanitary conditions that rivaled those of the Dark Ages.

Passengers were limited to two chests, no more than three and a half feet long, fifteen inches high, and seventeen wide—not much more than the two carry-on bags people used to be able to take onto an airplane. The decks were so crowded—with rigging, chain, cannon, anchors, gun carriages, coiled ropes, extra cargo, sleeping soldiers, off-duty sailors, spars, sails, and so many rats they ran off the ship's cats—that passengers could walk no more than twenty feet in any direction. And the deck was the place to be. Below was much worse.

A lot of people were on a galleon—at least when it set out. It wasn't uncommon for half of the three hundred to six hundred people who left Manila to die of disease, scurvy, thirst, or starvation before arriving in Mexico. Sometimes, they all died. In 1656, the *San Jose* appeared off Acapulco after more than a year at sea. It sent no signals and did not tack into the harbor but continued sailing south. When boats from Acapulco finally overtook her, they discovered a ship of mummies. Of the galleons that set out from Manila, thirty-three never made it. Of these, ten disappeared at "unknown locations." Given the prevailing winds and currents, it seems likely that a good portion went down along the coasts of Oregon and California.

As for what ship lies off Nehalem Spit, nobody knows. But the *St. Francis Xavier* would be a good guess. The *Xavier* was captained by Santiago Zabalburu, who was famous for overloading his ships. It disappeared in 1705, which meant it could have brought Soto's father to Oregon. Soto was the old man that Gabriel Franchere, one of John Jacob Astor's fur traders, found living in the Cascades claiming to be the son of a shipwrecked Spaniard.

Or, the ship might be the *San Augustin*. The *Augustin* was not one of the ten that disappeared at unknown locations. She wrecked somewhere on the coast of North America on November 30, 1595. The Spanish were sure about the date because the crew made it ashore and unloaded some of the cargo, stacking chests of silk and porcelain and tons of beeswax from the Philippines behind the dunes, before heading to Mexico in a launch. But even if it is the *Xavier* or the *San Augustin*, that doesn't mean there can't be other wrecks there as well.

Whichever ship is buried off Nehalem Spit, it is really buried, now. During the early twenties, the North Jetty was built to keep the spit from washing away, and the site began to sand up. What was left of the wreck was last spotted in 1929.

30

FOR WEEKS, I couldn't get the Siletz County grand jury off my mind. Every time somebody knocked on my door at home, or a stranger dropped by the office, I was sure I was about to be arrested. But time kept passing and nobody showed, and I let myself believe the DA had forgotten about indicting me and I began to worry more about what was going on at the office.

The day was coming when I would have to do something about Jolene. With Thaddeus Silk & Assoc. closing at the end of the year, she was going to have to come to an accommodation with her work-release program, or it was back to jail for her.

I told her I would take care of it. I figured that was the least I could do for somebody who had to spend her days listening to Tail Pipe confessing.

Tail Pipe was the Lawrence Welk of penitents, rerunning endless scenes of things so fanciful and so trivial and so long ago it was hard to believe anybody could ever have cared. But, if he wanted to make it to Step Six at Alcoholics Anonymous and have God come down and fix all his defects of character, he was going to have to get through Step Five and finish confessing. That's the way it works at AA, and Tail Pipe wasn't taking any chances—which meant a lot of repetition, because he was never quite sure what he had already owned up to.

"She left her bicycle in the bushes, and I . . . I . . . knew about all the terrible things that happen to bicycles in bushes, and I started thinking how if I really wanted to be her friend, I'd . . ." Tail Pipe faded out as he lost the thread of his confession. Luckily, Jolene had heard it before.

"Bicycle," she said helpfully.

"Hunh?"

"Bicycle," she repeated. "You were telling me about how you stole the little neighbor girl's bicycle."

"Bicycle?" Tail Pipe thought it over. "Was that the one she left in the bushes?"

"Yeah," Jolene said gently. "And you thought of all the terrible things that happen to bikes in bushes and—"

"How"—Tail Pipe sounded startled—"do you know about that?" He was quiet for a moment, as if thinking about all the ways Jolene could have found out, then remembered. "It was those cops in the office, wasn't it?"

"Cops?" Now it was her turn to be confused.

"They were all over the place, going through things." Tail Pipe thought about the cops going through things. "I think they were looking for something."

"You mean when Thaddeus died?" Jolene was starting to pick the thread of the conversation back up.

"Thaddeus died?" Tail Pipe began to cry at the idea Thaddeus had died.

Jolene put down her book on the history of the telegraph system in Great Britain and walked over and slipped her arm around him. "It's been a while, now."

"That's the kind of thing that happens . . . when you take somebody's . . . bicycle." Tail Pipe choked with guilt. "All I wanted was a bicycle of my own, so when I saw that poor bike left in the bushes like that I . . . I . . . and, now, Thaddeus is dead."

"How old," Jolene asked quietly, "were you?"

"How old was I when?"

"How old were you when you took that little girl's bicycle?"

"I was . . . I was . . . ," Tail Pipe muttered to himself, trying to figure out some way to calculate how old he had been that awful day. "I must have been seven because . . . I know she was six and she was a friend of my . . . cousin. My cousin was eight, and if he was eight, then . . . I'm the one who must have been six. At least, I guess I must of . . ." Tail Pipe faded out, again. He was not an efficient admitter.

As hard as Tail Pipe tried to confess, it was harder to imagine God was ever really going to come down and make it all better. As better as anything on this earth could make it, Jolene was already doing that. And he loved her for it with a fierceness that was hard to miss in a man otherwise so vague.

Keeping Jolene out of jail shouldn't have been much of a trick. She had already put in her work-release time, and the monthly reports had been filled out long ago. Thaddeus had just never sent them in. Like most things with Thaddeus Silk, I couldn't tell whether he wanted to keep a good thing going and sat on her paperwork or he was just sloppy.

Nobody goes to jail for shoplifting a couple of skirts. Jolene should have been plea-bargained to a few hours of community service, and that would have been that. But with Thaddeus Silk on the case, she was lucky she hadn't been put away for life. It was pure Thaddeus. He trashed her defense, then took her on as an indentured servant. Then he didn't file the papers that would have set her free. So, now, it was my turn to get her off the hook.

31

A S ABBY'S TRIAL approached, she and Shelley began spending a lot of time searching through the evidence against her, trying to discover some way to keep her out of jail.

Maybe looking at an endless stretch of hard time had inspired them. Or, maybe, there was just a lot of residual THC in Abby's bloodstream. In fact, the THC may not have been all that residual, at least if her straw bag was any indication. It still dribbled seeds across the carpet. And she still smelled of bad marijuana smoke.

"Here's the deal." She bounced into my office one morning with the goofy, hopeful look of a thirteen-year-old trying to talk her parents out of the car for the weekend. "Me and Shelley saw this movie about a dope dealer who cut a deal with the Feds where he told them who the players were and they dropped the charges and—"

"Just one thing," I told them. "It wasn't the Feds who busted you."

"That's the beauty of it." She fairly glowed with excitement. "When the state drops the charges, nobody will think the Feds had anything to do with it."

"That's because . . ." I tried to think of some way of putting this gently, then gave up. "The Feds won't have had anything to do with it."

"They will after you tell them what we got." Shelley crossed his arms firmly. "When the Feds want a case dropped, you better believe it gets dropped."

"When the state has a case in state court," I tried to explain, "the Feds don't have anything to do with it." But lectures on the separation of powers were lost on Shelley. He knew too much.

"When the Feds want something done," he explained back, "the states ask, 'How high?' Everybody knows that." There was no arguing with Shelley on that one. He had summed up the first semester of constitutional law about as neatly as I'd ever heard.

"And, then"—Abby came to the good part—"I can disappear into the Witness Protection Program."

The Witness Protection Program? "The Witness Protection Program is for gangsters."

"The Witness Protection Program," Shelley said, setting me straight, "is for witnesses who need protecting." When you came down to it, he knew as much about the Witness Protection Program as I did. We had seen the same movies. Still, I took a shot at explaining the system to him.

"The Witness Protection Program is for witnesses who need protecting in order to testify in federal court." That much I was pretty sure about. "Nobody wants Abby to testify anywhere." I didn't even want her testifying at her own trial.

"The Witness Protection Program is for people who have something the Feds want," Shelley said. "Testifying doesn't have anything to do with it."

Maybe he had watched more movies than I had. Whatever. I couldn't see why the federal government would care about Abby. "It's for people who need protecting from gangsters."

"Who do you think that dope belonged to?" Shelley asked. "You think it was a bunch of schoolkids out there on Neahkahnie Beach that night with four and a half tons of—"

"One and a half," Abby interrupted softly. "It was one and a half tons."

"One and a half tons of dope," Shelley went on. "You think those people would just forget about a thing like that?"

"And, now . . ." Abby bit her lip, trying not to cry. "It's been on the radio and they know exactly where it went and my only chance is to disappear into the Witness Protection Program and . . ."

And I felt a twinge of guilt over it. More than a twinge, actually, since I was the one who had blown her cover. "And you think you know something the Feds want bad enough to—"

"I know who"—Abby looked hopeful, again—"was behind the dope drops in Siletz County."

"You know who the gangsters are?" I wasn't sure I wanted to get mixed up in this any more than I already had. The movies hadn't mentioned anything about protection programs for lawyers.

"I know who Sheriff High Hand was."

"High Hand?" *The sheriff who used to be half a partner in the SurfSea Tavern?*

"Of course High Hand," Shelley said. "You think anybody could run that much dope through a county unless the sheriff was in on it?"

"And now you think all you have to do is—" I definitely did not want anything to do with this harebrained scheme.

"The thing is," Shelley interrupted, "what other plans you got? Abby's going to jail on this one, big time. And, once they've got her locked up with gangsters, she's—"

"Dead meat," Abby broke in. "That's all I am. Dead meat unless you cut a deal with the Feds and get me disappeared."

They may have been right. They probably were right, for all I knew. The idea made sense in a movie-plot kind of way. Only it wasn't going to work.

"You think Abby can waltz up to the Feds and talk them into pressuring the Siletz County district attorney into forgetting about the biggest drug bust in the history of the Oregon Coast, maybe in the history of the world, just to get her to tell them about Sheriff High Hand?"

"We were hoping," Abby said hopefully, "that you would waltz them into it. And then I"—she spun happily around, as if it were already a done deal—"will disappear into the Witness Protection Program," and she did a ponderous pirouette across the office.

32

I N THE LAND of Fresh out of Ideas, the half-baked scheme is king. And ideas don't come any more half-baked than they do when cooked up by Abby and Shelley.

The problem was, Abby and Shelley were the only ones on our side of the case with any ideas at all—at least in the how-to-keep-Abby-out-of-jail-for-the-rest-of-her-life department. So I owed it to her—I owed it to the legal profession and justice, itself—to see if I couldn't get her disappeared into the Witness Protection Program. At least, that's what I tell myself every time I think about what happened in the DEA office. No matter how much the interest of justice demanded I go talk to the Drug Enforcement Administration, or how guilty I felt about getting Abby arrested, I should have thought it through a little more. In the first place . . .

"What makes you think the DEA has anything to do with the Witness Protection Program?" a grandmotherly woman with cutesy knick-knacks wanted to know. She had a Hummel figurine on the corner of her desk, and a whole collection of the overweight little ceramic villagers on her credenza. The figurine on her desk was a plump toddler in lederhosen standing next to a child-size wishing well and an equally plump little girl in a dirndl.

I wound up in her office, staring at those Hummel figurines, because I wasn't sure whom to ask for. "May I see the agent responsible for cutting undisclosed deals with underworld snitches?" didn't sound like something that would get me past the receptionist. So I hemmed and hawed and shuffled my feet and asked to meet the person in charge of the Oregon Coast.

I suppose there probably was somebody in charge of the Oregon Coast, drug-enforcement-wise—or the Pacific Northwest, or the Western states, or some such geographical area—but he was out. And, I got the distinct impression, he was going to stay out for "approximately the rest of your career practicing law, if you know what I mean, so if you want to actually talk to somebody, I suggest you make an appointment with the grandmotherly woman with the cutesy knick-knacks. It's up to you, I don't care one way or the other," or words to that effect. So, two weeks later, I found myself back in the federal building staring at a Hummel figurine trying to explain why I thought the DEA had anything to do with the Witness Protection Program.

I didn't sound all that convincing, even to me. It's just that I thought, well, the DEA was part of the government, and everybody knew the government was in charge of disappearing people into the Witness Protection Program. I tried to sound official and knowing and pompous in a lawyerly sort of way as I explained it, but that's what it came down to.

The grandmotherly lady sat back and stared at me.

Then she sat forward and began arranging papers on her desk to let me know that the interview was coming to a rapid conclusion. So I did what lawyers are trained to do in that kind of situation. I babbled.

I babbled about the Oregon Coast and Abby Birdsong and how she had stumbled onto all that dope over on Neahkahnie Beach and that she used to be a logger before she got caught up in the choker cable and then helped out a little at the SurfSea Tavern and . . .

And it must have worked, because when I said the thing about the SurfSea Tavern, the DEA lady stopped fiddling with her papers and started looking at me as if she was actually listening. Then she picked up the phone and called somebody. "Just a minute," she said, and stood and left the office.

It turned out to be a pretty long minute—about half an hour's worth. If I'd been almost anywhere else, I would have gotten up and walked around and checked out the wallpaper. But that morning, after I had babbled about the Oregon Coast and drug dealers nobody had ever seen, my judgment finally woke up and stretched and yawned and noticed where I was and snapped to attention and ordered me to stay put. Then, its duty done, it went back to sleep, and I got up and had a good look at what was on the walls.

She had a master's degree, in some kind of fancy, Gothic script, that might have been from Pepperdine. It was hard to tell because the college had translated its name into the trumped-up sort of Latin they supposed Goths would have used if the Goths had gotten it into their heads to name a college Pepperdine and wanted to do it in Latin. She had a couple of framed letters that turned out to be commendations, and a huge relief map of Oregon that took up most of one wall. The map was fitted together out of twelve-by-eighteen-inch molded panels that let you run your finger over the contours of plastic river valleys and buttes and high deserts. The Columbia curled along the top, and white, starfish shapes danced down the left where glaciers spangled the Cascades. Neahkahnie Mountain was there where I could touch it. And Short Sands Beach and Nehalem Spit. It was a beautiful map. I wanted one.

One of the commendations had something to do with a cache of drugs in a commercial wishing well south of Mount Angel. Weeks after the meeting, it occurred to me that the chubby kid in the lederhosen might not have had anything to do with cutesy. He might have been a trophy. Since then, I have spent a lot of time trying to remember the figurines on the credenza. The only one I am sure about was a little boy with a popgun and a puppy. If that was a trophy, too, I have no idea what the grandmotherly lady did to earn it.

When she came back, she laid a yellow pad with notes in tidy, government handwriting onto her desk and sat down. "One," she started without any kind of prologue, "we are not in the business of putting people into the Witness Protection Program, so you can forget about that.

"And, two," she ticked off the next point, "even if we were in the business of putting people into the Witness Protection Program, which we are not, I wouldn't be the one you would go to about it, if you get my drift."

"Well, if you aren't the one"—I thought I was getting her drift—"then who would I . . ."

"Nobody." She smiled. "I told you. We aren't in the business of putting people into the Witness Protection Program. Now, three, nobody needs protecting, anymore. Do you have any *idea* what the life span of a drug runner is? Two . . . three years . . . tops. Whoever your client stole that dope from ten years ago is no threat to anybody, now."

I don't know how the DEA lady could have been so sure about that, but it was pretty clear she wasn't talking statistical probabilities. When she said those people weren't a threat anymore, she knew.

"It's not the drug runners." I tried to come up with something to make her want to deal. "It's the elected officials who let—"

"Which brings me to four. In case you haven't gotten the word," she gave me the word, "Sheriff High Hand isn't a threat to anybody anymore, either."

The air kind of ran out of me at that. High Hand's name was the only thing Abby had to sell to the DEA, and the DEA already had it. Even if the grandmotherly lady had been bluffing about everything else, Abby wasn't going to be able to cut a deal because Abby didn't have anything to deal with. But the grandmotherly lady hadn't been bluffing. I was the one who had been bluffing, as I was about to find out.

"And, five. Nothing ever happened at the SurfSea. Those rumors have been going around for years and you can forget about them." Then, she leaned forward and spoke precisely to make sure I understood what she was getting at. "This isn't on my list, but, six, you look like a nice enough young man. A word to the wise. It's not in the interest of your client . . . it's not in your interest . . . to try to blackmail the federal government by dredging up rumors from long ago that are best left not dredged up." Then she sat back in her chair, all smiles, as if that ended the matter.

And it might have, too, if I'd had any idea what she was talking about. Whatever made her think I was trying to blackmail the government was beyond me.

A few minutes later, while I was driving back to the office, it occurred to me that Abby and Shelley would know what she had been talking about. They were the ones, I realized, who had sent me down there to blackmail the government in the first place.

33

I T TURNED OUT Abby and Shelley hadn't just been innocently looking at the moon the night they'd heard gunshots on Neahkahnie Beach. They'd been waiting out there for something to happen. It's just that more happened than they had been waiting for. "It was"—she sniffled—"the *federales*." She sniffled, again.

"Hold *on*," I interrupted. "You are talking about *federal* agents? You never mentioned federal agents before."

"Yeah," she said in a tiny voice. "DEA guys. At least I think they were DEA. Nobody really knew who they were, except they were *federales*. They would come in the SurfSea and drink and wait for calls, and there was this one guy who talked too much and—"

"You were drinking with federal agents?"

"No. I mean, yes. Sometimes. We all were. I was waiting tables. Okay? And there weren't any other pay phones in town, so they had to hang around the SurfSea if they were expecting a call and . . ."

These must have been the guys nobody recognized, the guys Thaddeus told me about. Only, they hadn't been gangsters at all. They had been federal agents.

"They had this system. When a dope drop was about to go down, somebody would call and tell them. We weren't supposed to know about that, but I spent a lot of time back of the bar pulling beers and couldn't help overhearing when people talked on the phone."

"You're trying to tell me federal agents were running marijuana?"

"No. Well, they weren't supposed to. This was in '71. Nixon hated drugs and he had these special teams go out and meet the shipments right on the beach. But they must have had a piece of

173

the action behind Nixon's back because nobody ever seemed to get busted."

"You believed this?"

"Everybody did. Besides, Shelley was a deputy, and he wasn't allowed anywhere near the beach some nights. Whatever was going on out there, the locals were supposed to stay out of it."

"So . . ." This was making less and less sense. "What were you doing screwing with Shelley up on Neahkahnie Beach the night you found the dope?"

"We weren't fucking." She looked truly hurt that I'd think something like that. "We were at the SurfSea when this call came and the *federales* sauntered out like nothing was going on, so everybody knew something big was about to happen. Besides"—she thought it over—"word was out in the sheriff's department not to go to Neahkahnie Beach that night. So when those *federales* took off, me and Shelley thought it would be a hoot to go up and see where all the dope came from. Anyway, they must have had to stop for their guns or something because we got there first.

"We found a dark place in the dunes, and after a while we heard a boat coming in from the ocean. Only it turned out to be different from what we expected. The *federales* hadn't come for the dope. They let the guys who brought it in unload the whole stash, then they blew them away and left their bodies right there on the sand. There were three of them. I guess what they say about Nixon was right. He really did hate drugs."

"You're telling me," I asked her, "federal agents go around at night and shoot people and leave the bodies on the beach?" No wonder the DEA lady thought I had been trying to blackmail the government.

"Not exactly. They had this earthmoving company down in Lantern Rock come and bury—"

"An earthmoving company?"

"They'd call this guy when they needed him, and he'd come and dispose of the evidence right there under the sand. But Lantern Rock isn't anywhere near Neahkahnie, so it took a while before he showed up, and, by then, the *federales* were long gone and me and Shelley had loaded Susie B. and were out of there, too." She even knew the date.

"Well, not exactly the date," she said. "But I know when it was. It was the time Grady Jackson got thrown off the beach for digging at night. All that noise the earthmoving guy made burying the bodies, the neighbors thought it was Grady running his backhoe, and they turned him in and . . ."

It was a wonder the DEA lady hadn't had me killed.

34

GRADY NOW HAD not just one, but two eyewitnesses to the fact that, no matter how much pressure the Department of Justice was bringing on the DA, he couldn't have dug up the chain the night he was kicked off Neahkahnie Beach, because Grady Jackson hadn't been the one who was digging out there that night. It was the killer alibi Lydia had wanted. It even involved real killers.

The only problem was, being eyewitnesses at Grady's trial was the one thing Abby and Shelley could never do, not without putting themselves in jail on the very marijuana charges I was supposed to be defending Abby against. And, most likely, as accessories to the murders they had witnessed but hadn't mentioned to anybody for a decade or so.

I couldn't even use what I knew to keep myself out of jail—not without putting the finger on Abby, which I could not do because I wasn't just Grady's lawyer, I was her lawyer, too. I felt like a priest in a Catholic-exploitation movie who has to keep his mouth shut about the atom bomb ticking away beneath the Vatican because he heard about it in confession.

35

A FEW DAYS later, Abby and Shelley were back in my office with a new crackpot scheme to keep her out of jail for the rest of her life.

"This is it," she chortled. "We can prove the sheriff is lying. See?" She pointed at one of the big, glossy photographs of the four and a half tons of decaying marijuana the sheriff had found in her storage locker.

She and Shelley had the pictures laid out on a worktable in a complicated grid pattern that let them see every single collapsing bale of dope she had once owned. "You just look at these. There's not even a ton and a half in here." Her long, unbraided hair shifted loosely across her back, then fell from her shoulders as she leaned onto the table.

"More like twenty-eight hundred pounds." Shelley waved a tidy accounting sheet covered with little tick marks. "This is it, babe. The moment that sheriff tries to tell the jury you had four and a half tons, we bust him for perjury, the case against you falls apart, and he's the one who goes down." He gave Abby a huge, sprawling hug.

Watching Abby and Shelley spin ever loopier plans to keep her out of jail, I began to wonder whether you could plead drug-induced insanity as a defense in a dope case.

"I'm clean, I'm clean. The photos prove I'm clean." Abby did a little pirouette, spinning her hair in a gorgeous, swirling cloud of femininity that was eye-catching, even on her. Then she danced a ponderous dance over to the Xerox machine—evidence as good as that needed to be reproduced—and almost danced into Mr. Beefy Bad Rocco Cop and his partner, Ms. Velvet Blond Good Cop.

Sometimes I missed Sophie. There was no way a pair of cops, good or bad, or anybody else, could have gotten into the office unannounced with Sophie Silk sitting guard out front. Luckily, they hadn't come for Abby.

They had come to find out where Thaddeus kept the things he wanted to keep private. And to remind me they were still on the case and were going to get to the bottom of it, regardless of whether I took their lie-detector test. But the sight of Abby Birdsong pirouetting across the office wrapped in a cloud of stale marijuana fumes was enough to make them reconsider their mission.

"You"—she waved the accounting sheet at the two cops—"better start looking for work because I'm going to blow the lid off this town." That the little tick marks Shelley had made were about dope in an entirely different county didn't dampen her opinion of their employment prospects. "Blow the lid off." She giggled and began making copies.

As unobtrusively as I could, I dropped her straw purse into a file drawer. That way I could claim it was private legal documents, or work product, or attorney-client-privileged, or some other damn thing long enough to make Rocco and Velvet go for a warrant while I figured out something better to do with it. I think I had the drawer closed before Rocco noticed what I was doing.

"She is . . . ?" he gestured in Abby's direction.

"Clean." Abby giggled as she spun past the Xerox machine. "Not a scrap of dope on me. That's for sure." It was almost enough to get her strip-searched.

"I'm clean and good and pure and true," Abby began to sing. "I did no harm to—" Whom or whatever it was she did no harm to, I never found out because Shelley slipped his hand over her mouth and sat her down next to Tail Pipe.

"Your client?" Rocco asked in his most authoritative voice.

"Damn straight," I said, scuffing my shoe over the place her straw bag had been, trying to rub the marijuana seeds into the cheap carpet.

"And, let me point out that telling you she is clean is not probable cause to pat her down for dope."

"Clean. She's clean . . ." Tail Pipe picked up the tune in his cracked baritone, then noticed the two police officers for the first time, decided they had come about the stolen bicycle, and sank back into his chair.

"Mind if we take another look around Mr. Silk's office?" Velvet changed the subject with a sweet smile.

"Okay by me," I said. As a lawyer, I was pretty sure it wasn't supposed to be okay. But, when I thought about it, I couldn't come up with a good reason why not, not as many times as that office had already been searched. I followed them in.

They poked through the boxes I had sorted Thaddeus's files into, but their hearts weren't in it. After a while, Rocco made a show of walking over to the desk and picking up the tape recorder attached to the phone. Then he scowled at me and wanted to know, "Where are the tapes Mr. Silk made on this . . . thing?" He looked as if it were a real struggle to keep from turning me upside down and shaking the tapes out of my pockets.

I had no idea.

"Well, if you ever do figure out what's going on around here"—he glared at me—"you've got my card." As he and Velvet turned to leave, she gave me another of her disappointed looks and they were out the door, and gone.

"Love Nest," Jolene said shyly, a few minutes later. "Thaddeus kept the tapes at his Secret Love Nest. There's a safe up there. They should have asked me."

She wrote the address on a phone slip. "A client wanted us to keep an eye on his cabin for him." She dropped her eyes for a moment. "I don't think he's coming back."

"Safes," Tail Pipe snorted, and began to rise out of his chair. "She knows how to open safes. Jolene knows how to . . . she . . . can . . ." Tail Pipe lost the thread of what he was saying and sank back into his chair.

"Is that true?" I asked Jolene. "Can you open that safe up there?"

She nodded, and it took me less than a second to realize we were going to the Love Nest.

And, about another second to realize she and I weren't going alone. Shelley grabbed the phone slip, and he and Abby were out the door before we were.

36

THE LOVE NEST turned out to be a log cabin overlooking Zigzag Creek on the west slope of Mt. Hood. We got there by taking Highway 26, swinging north onto Hummingbird, then along a rutted Forest Service road through dark, moss-hung trees. And that's where the Love Nest stayed for the next twenty-some years.

It would still be there if I hadn't driven up that way recently and noticed Hummingbird Road is on the south side of 26. So, the Love Nest must actually have been off Sleepy Hollow Lane.

That's what happens when you leave your subconscious in charge of the record-keeping. You check in later and discover that the humdrum biography that actually happened has been swapped for glittering never-weres that dance and sparkle in your memory to form your who-you-ares. So, it's not that I don't vouch for what comes next. I'm going to set it down exactly as I remember it. It's just that what went on that evening at the Love Nest may come out a little more dramatic than if somebody other than my subconscious had been responsible for keeping the facts pruned into shape. But, then, the memory of Tail Pipe with a .50-caliber rifle would distort a place in anybody's recollection.

It had just stopped raining when he and Jolene and I pulled into the little clearing. Susie B. was already there, decked out with a light-bar on top, and Shelley's custom-built .50-caliber rifle in the gun rack. He and Abby were in the cabin and the lights were on. The door hadn't been locked. There wouldn't have been any point. Back in the trees a burglar, or a lost hunter, has all the time in the world, so owners save wear and tear by leaving their places open.

The Love Nest had the look of Thaddeus Silk about it. It was rumpled and messy and came with a wonderful collection of LP jazz records. The living area had a huge rock fireplace at one end, with andirons made from lengths of railroad track. Dozens of expensive liquor bottles lined the stone mantel, and a massive billiards table sat in the middle of the room. Outside, the trees and ferns dripped and splashed and glowed with a late-afternoon green that could have been a thousand miles from Portland, and centuries, too, it felt that remote out there.

The little propane stove in the kitchen had two burners, the sink was rust-stained from the dripping tap, three cast-iron skillets hung from the ceiling, enamel-ware plates were stacked on the counter, and a lot more whiskey glasses than juice glasses were in the cabinet. Sheets were wadded at the foot of one of the bunks in the tiny bedroom. Washing sheets was one more thing Thaddeus got out of by having a heart attack.

The safe was hidden behind a big, 1950s wet bar, but Jolene knew where to go. She walked over and sank into the lotus position and began twisting the dial.

And nothing happened.

It turned out that knowing how to open a safe wasn't the same as knowing the combination to that safe, at least as far as Jolene was concerned. As far as Jolene was concerned, all you needed to open a safe was a safe, and a little know-how. The know-how came from an article she'd once read about how to crack safes.

According to the article, there's enough leeway built into the dial on a safe that you don't have to get the numbers exactly right. Two numbers either way works just as well. So, if one of the numbers is 5, anything from 3 all the way to 7 will do. Which means that, rather than having to turn the dial 100 x 100 x 100, or a million, times to go through all the combinations, a clever burglar, meaning Jolene, only has 20 x 20 x 20 possibilities, and cracking a safe is a snap. At least the article made it sound like a snap to anybody who hadn't multiplied those twenties together. Reading too many articles is the curse of the informal education.

While we waited, Abby plumped onto a sofa for a relaxing toke. Tail Pipe dragged a big, overstuffed chair around the end of the bar where he could gaze lovingly as Jolene worked her way through the eight thousand possible combinations. And Shelley, well, Shelley was stoked by the whole idea of a secret cabin and walked outside to check on the hydraulic possibilities of Zigzag Creek.

A few minutes later, he burst back in, dancing with fire and enthusiasm. "It's off the grid," he told us. "This whole place is off the grid."

Actually, he was wrong about that. The cabin was on the grid. The power company had seen to that by running a drop from the main feed along Highway 26. It was the reason he and Abby had been able to flick on the lights when they'd arrived. But Shelley wasn't thinking about what was. Shelley was thinking possibilities, and the possibilities were huge.

"We put in a waterwheel down there and it's Good-bye, Power Company. And it's not just electricity." Shelley went into a paroxysm of rapture, as if he were explaining to a judge that he wasn't required to pay taxes because money hadn't been legal tender since the government did away with the gold standard. "It's gas . . . it's water. No going hat in hand to the utility companies, here. We just put in a pipe and—"

"I kind of like the water company." Abby shifted her bulk on the sofa. "I mean, they put all that water into the other end of a pipe, and it comes out right in your tub and all you've got to do is . . ." She had an almost defiant look. "It's not like I enjoy paying the bill and all, but . . ."

"It's not the bill that's the problem," Shelley snorted. "It's the way they get your name in their computer, and every time you jump, the Man in Whiskers knows right where you land." The Man in Whiskers was what Shelley called the shadowy cabal of government officials who ran the world. "But out here"—he waved at the trees through the window—"he forgets all about you and—"

"I think," Abby said in a small voice, "it's national forest out here."

"National forest?" Shelley said to himself. "Government land." He began to grin. If you were off the grid out here, you were off the grid on government land. The idea of free citizens colonizing federal land appealed to Shelley.

"Seven . . . twenty-two . . ." Over by the safe, Jolene was keeping track of the combinations. ". . . twelve."

"With a place like this," Shelley said, "you could—"

"Hunt," Tail Pipe said from the overstuffed chair at the end of the bar. "You could . . . you could . . ."

"Hunt?" Jolene reminded him sweetly from the floor.

"Yeah," Tail Pipe said, grateful to his woman for saving him one more embarrassment. "You could hunt."

"Hunt works," Shelley agreed. "If you live off the grid, you got to eat."

"Love nest." Abby giggled. "It works for a love nest."

"Love nest?" Tail Pipe looked as if he was trying to put together another thought. "Love nest?" Then he lost hold and sank back into the overstuffed chair.

I tried to imagine where Thaddeus took his girlfriends when they came up. Abby's couch, perhaps. Or the bunk with the sheets pulled off. Somehow it was hard to imagine Thaddeus and a . . .

"Love Nest." Tail Pipe struggled to sit up. "Love Nest . . ." Something was just beneath the surface of his consciousness. Something that reminded him of . . .

"Twelve . . . two—" Jolene counted softly to herself, "thirty-seven."

"Love Nest!" Tail Pipe climbed to his feet. "Love Nest!" He wobbled a little and stumbled to the door and turned and pointed at Jolene. "Love Nest!" he shouted, and blundered out into the gathering darkness.

"Love Nest . . . *Love Nest* . . . love nest . . ." His boots made little scribbling sounds against the gravel as he stumbled across the clearing on some mission.

I think if Jolene hadn't been so wrapped up in doing the right thing with that safe, she might have seen what was coming. I could have seen it, too, but I was slow. It was another few seconds before it occurred to me Tail Pipe might have noticed the same thing I'd noticed when we'd come in—that Jolene had known exactly where the safe was, just as if she had been up to Thaddeus's love nest before.

Lights from outside dazzled into the cabin.

"Get away from the safe," the mechanical sound of a bullhorn bellowed at us. At first, I thought it was the police, that somehow—

"Get away from . . . get away . . ." And lost the train of thought. It was Tail Pipe.

He was in Susie B. He had the headlights and the light-bar, both, blasting into the window of the cabin. He had the bullhorn. And he seemed unusually focused on whatever he had in mind.

"I've got the . . ." Tail Pipe trailed off as the metallic sound of a round chambering into a rifle cut through the cabin. "I've got . . . got . . ."

"The fifty-caliber," Shelley yelled.

With the right ammunition, that rifle would put one hell of a hole through something a lot tougher and meaner than Jolene. Thirteen years earlier, when Uncle had gotten it into his head that I was just the guy to bring peace and freedom to Vietnam, I'd had my chance to study .50-caliber weapons as up close and as personal as I cared to get. At a mile, a .50-caliber will punch a hole through an armored personnel carrier. And, now, somewhere outside, Tail Pipe was waving a .50-caliber rifle in—

BLAAAAMMMMMM.

Glass and expensive liquor and sharp fragments of cedar and basalt flew across the room as one of the big fireplace rocks exploded. Shelley had the right ammunition, all right.

"Tail Pipe," we all yelled. "Tail—"

BLAAAAAMMM.

A skillet slammed across the kitchen.

"—*Pipe.*"

By then we were all grabbing the floor like actors in a war movie. Outside, we could hear Tail Pipe chambering another . . .

"Tail Pipe! For—"

BLAAAAMMMMM.

Burners flew into the air, the stove skidded over the linoleum, the oven popped open, and I worried about whether the propane was turned off.

"Jolene?" I asked as quietly as I could manage in the circumstances. "Jolene, you okay?" I wondered whether we could get her out a back window and into the woods without somebody being—

BLAAAAMMMMMMMMMMM.

In the bedroom, mattresses pancaked to the floor as the end blew off one of the bunks. Tail Pipe didn't seem to have a steady aim.

"How many?" Abby yelled from behind the sofa. "How many bullets did you—"

BLAAAAAAMMMMM.

CLAAANNNₙₙₙₙGGG.

CLAAAANNNNNNNGGGGGGGGGGG.

Enamel-coated metal plates ricocheted off the walls and onto the floor.

BLAAAAAAMMMₘₘₘₘₘ.

The heavy billiards table swung to the side and collapsed as one of its legs shattered.

"Just the usual." Shelley low-crawled through broken glass, sharp bits of rock, and splinters of cedar log. "Maybe six thousand—"

Blaaaammmmmmmmmmmmmmmmmm.

"Six thousand . . . bullets?" Jolene yelled in astonishment. "Tail Pipe's got six thousand bullets for that . . . that—"

Blaaaaammmmmm.

Nothing happened. Tail Pipe must have missed the cabin entirely.

Blaaaaammm.

The front door collapsed as the top hinge blew off. I wondered if Tail Pipe could see Jolene through the opening. It was time to get her out of here.

"Jolene," I said as quietly as I could. "After the next shot. Before he can re—"

Blaaaaaammmmmmmmmm.

An andiron flew across the room. The railroad track was blown through with a jagged hole.

"*Now, Jolene, now now now.*"

"Oh, *alright*," she said, and stood up and walked to the door. "Tail Pipe. You put that thing—"

Blaaaaammmmmmmmm.

Followed by a sound that could only have been a large tree crashing to the ground.

"Tail Pipe!" she yelled again, and stepped out into the glare of the lights.

"Yeah, babe?" he yelled back. "Did I get it?"

When she returned, Tail Pipe stood behind her, a dark, hulking shadow in the glare from Susie B.

"He couldn't hear." She stared at her feet as if it were all her fault. "He was inside Abby's truck, and once he fired that first shot, he was, like, you know. That gun's loud and he was deaf from the noise so he couldn't hear what we were yelling and all he wanted to do was—"

"Awwwwww," he said as he got a good look at the safe. "I didn't hit it even once?" He looked as if he wanted to cry. Just one more defeat.

"Do you have any idea what this is going to cost?" Shelley kicked his way through the wreckage to reclaim his rifle.

"He knew I was having trouble with the combination," Jolene said. "And he . . . well, he's such a dear, he didn't want me to be embarrassed, and all that talk about love nests made him think how much he loved me, and he knew Shelley's gun was out there and he thought he would give me a hand, only out in Susie B. he didn't have such a good line on where the safe was, so he just tried to home in on it by dead reckoning. Isn't that right?"

Tail Pipe shuffled a bit and nodded.

"I lost my place." Jolene gave Tail Pipe a reassuring squeeze on the arm to let him know everything was okay, then turned back to the safe. "I'm going to have to start over."

"Do you have any idea what this is going to cost?" Shelley propped his rifle against the remains of the billiard table. "That Browning machine-gun ammunition you were making so free with ain't cheap."

"Two . . . ," Jolene said as she started over, "two . . . two."

Then Shelley brightened up. "See? See what I told you? A place like this, you can do whatever you want. Even"—he looked at the safe—"blow open a safe with a fifty-caliber rifle."

It took a lot of grunting to get the safe outside. It must have weighed six hundred pounds, but we couldn't get a clean shot at it through the window, and nobody but Tail Pipe was willing to stand inside and pull the trigger. And none of the rest of us were willing to let Tail Pipe anywhere near the .50-caliber again.

From about a hundred yards, Shelley put a hole the size of a quarter through the door of the safe, and a jagged opening out the back big enough to drop a tennis ball through. And the bullet kept going, so we couldn't tell where it stopped, if it ever did. But, the safe was still locked.

The second shot blew right through the dial. When we went to check, wet ground was covered with twenty-dollar bills and the door was wrenched back so far the hinges were bent and we couldn't get it shut again.

There had probably been a thousand twenties in there. It was hard to tell, exactly. Half were so shot-up you couldn't spend them anymore, and I'm not sure we even found most of them. It was dark and wet, and they were scattered all over the place. And only Shelley and Abby and I actually looked. Tail Pipe had been overcome by the guilts for taking Shelley's rifle without asking, and Jolene had to listen to him confess about it.

There turned out to be something in the safe that the bullets had missed: a cigar box of microcassettes from the recorder hooked up to Thaddeus's phone, all neatly labeled with names. I counted twenty-nine, and I would have laid odds Thaddeus could have reached into that box and pulled out a tape for anybody in his life he wanted something from.

37

AS FAR AS I was concerned, the grand jury could have picked a better time to talk to Jolene and Tail Pipe about the stolen treasure, but they didn't ask my opinion. The morning after we got back from shooting up Thaddeus's Secret Love Nest, the subpoenas arrived.

It was hard to imagine what course justice might take once seven citizens, good and true, had a chance to pick those two brains, and I tried to coach them on what was at stake. But it didn't take. Knowing when to keep your mouth shut, and when to plead the Fifth, only works when you have a basic idea what's likely to get somebody in trouble.

Gentle, sweet Jolene didn't have a clue.

And Tail Pipe couldn't move past the part about taking the Fifth. Every time I brought it up, he got a hurt look and said, "Not me. I never took no fifth." Then he would go on about admitting to God and himself and another human being, and how he knew better than to take things, and even if he didn't, he still wouldn't take anybody's fifths because he had plenty of money to buy his own.

I'm not sure what either of them actually told the grand jury, because I had to wait in the hall while they told it. One thing district attorneys do not need is some lawyer sitting next to witnesses advising them what their rights are. If you're lucky, he will let the witnesses come out in the hall and ask you questions, sometimes. But for the entire eight-hour day I sat outside the Siletz County grand-jury room, neither Tail Pipe nor Jolene ever came out and asked anything.

The day wasn't completely wasted, though. Around the middle of the afternoon, I got a message from somebody pretty high up. A deputy drifted by to deliver it. "You that lawyer?" he asked as he took a seat on the bench next to me.

I nodded. It was warm and I'd had a crab sandwich for lunch and I was feeling sleepy.

"Swiped the brooch?"

Suddenly I was wide-awake. Whatever this deputy had in mind, it wasn't just to chat.

"Thought so." He grinned. "You represent Mr. Jackson . . . Grady, isn't it? Used to run that bar over in Frenchman's Cove?"

I didn't see where saying anything was going to help me or Grady, so I kept as much of a poker face as I could manage and waited for the deputy to fill me in on where this was going. And, he did.

"Arlene and I used to go there, sometimes. Nice place. Nobody wants to see anything happen to Grady. Just tell him to turn over the treasure and this whole thing blows over. Hell"—he grinned at me— "they may even let you keep the brooch, for all I know."

We sat for a bit, and I still didn't say anything.

After a while, he started back into his prepared monologue. "The thing you got to remember is, bullshit as those sunken-treasure charges may be, the DA knows the jurors down here a lot better than you do. If he ever gets that case in front of a jury, somebody's going to jail. Maybe more than one somebody, if you take my meaning." He smiled, as if he was certain I took his meaning.

"You and Mr. Jackson"—his message almost delivered, the deputy stood to leave—"are the only ones can turn this off." And he headed down the hall and was gone.

Hours later, when Jolene finally emerged back into the light of day, she told me what had gone on in the grand-jury room. She thought the DA had been nice. He asked a lot of questions about Thaddeus and what happened at the office and what Sophie did and what I did, and she answered as best she could, but she hadn't gotten any of us in trouble, she was sure about that. I was sure the DA would let me know just how much trouble Jolene hadn't gotten me into when the time came.

192

Tail Pipe was pumped by the whole experience. He went into the grand-jury room and admitted to God and to himself and to seven grand jurors, one district attorney, and a court reporter, who copied down every word, the exact nature of how he'd gone up to Zigzag Creek and shot up a cabin. He named the date and the location as best he could. He also named names. And, he got the names right. He knew he got the names right because he saw those people around the office every day. Tail Pipe couldn't wait to get down to AA and tell everybody how well he had done.

Somehow, I'd gotten myself mixed up in a crime even Thaddeus hadn't managed to commit. Quite an accomplishment.

38

A COUPLE OF days later, Lydia Stonemason called with the latest scoop from deep inside the grand-jury room. The good news was, I hadn't been indicted for shooting up the cabin at Zigzag Creek.

Lydia didn't even know what that was about. "The DA kept trying to get somebody named Tail Pipe to blow the whistle on you for fencing stolen treasure, but all he seemed to want to do was confess."

It had started out pretty much as I'd expected. Tail Pipe had walked into the grand-jury room and admitted to God, himself, and nine other human beings what had happened at Zigzag Creek. The grand jurors were courteous people, and conscientious, and seemed to listen carefully, at least as far as you can tell from the transcript Lydia had somehow gotten hold of, but they never quite got a fix on the exact nature of the wrongs Tail Pipe had committed. Other people on some other grand jury might have figured it out, but you can't listen to what's in the transcript of this grand jury without getting the feeling that these particular people concluded early on that subpoenaing Tail Pipe had been a mistake.

The transcript is filled with polite remarks about how terrible the grand jurors felt about his belly button, and if he would only be a little more specific about this Charlie person, they would ask the DA to look into the shooting. But, for now, they were just glad he was safe, and he should really be careful next time not to zig when he was supposed to zag, and, yes, they could tell what a sweet girl Jolene was, and they knew he would never take anybody's whiskey no matter what those lawyers tried to make him do, and they would be sure to call him if they needed anything else, which they probably wouldn't because he had been so helpful already.

"Do you have any idea what that's about?" Lydia sounded uncharacteristically puzzled, now that she'd had a chance to read through the transcript, again.

I didn't, at least not that I wanted to share, and she just let the whole thing go as the inexplicable ramblings of a drunk. Besides, she still had the bad news to tell me about. The bad news was, the grand jury had indicted me weeks ago for conspiracy to fence stolen treasure. The only reason I hadn't been arrested was that the old judge in Siletz County had been sitting on the warrant.

"He knows it's bullshit," Lydia told me. "He's had it on his desk for weeks. But he's not going to be able to hold off signing forever. The Department of Justice is bringing too much pressure, and the moment he signs, you can bet the DA is going to hand-carry the warrant to Multnomah County and have you arrested the same day." She paused for a moment. "The best thing would be to cut a deal."

Deal? "You mean, agree to go to prison over some kind of reduced sentence just to get out of . . . ?"

"I think I could get you probation. The DA doesn't want you. He wants the treasure. And a jury is always a crapshoot."

"The problem is"—I tried to think this through—"I don't have any treasure to give him. I don't even know about any treasure."

"Except that gold chain, but Grady got that from the king of Arabia," she said in the sarcastic voice the DA was sure to use when he discussed that particular excuse with the jury. She didn't need to mention the emerald brooch that had disappeared the night Thaddeus died. Or the other things that had been in his safe. "It's up to you." She paused, as if waiting to see whether I had any second thoughts about what I wanted to tell her about the treasure. "I don't think the case against you is a winner. I feel reasonably confident we can beat it at trial. Sixty percent. But a jury is a crapshoot for us, too. And there's something else you need to think about."

Something *else?*

"The conflict of interest with Grady Jackson. Right now, you don't

196

have any way of knowing what went on in that grand-jury room, so you don't have a conflict of interest. But you will."

I could see where this was going. The moment I was served with the warrant, I would have to resign as Grady's lawyer. Once two people are accused of the same crime, they need to be able to point the finger at each other to save their own butts.

That would leave me in a real pickle. If I had to resign as Grady's lawyer, there wouldn't be any more wads of cash slipped to me under the counsel table. Even if I could figure out how to live off the spotty payments Abby Birdsong sometimes sent my way, I sure wouldn't be able to pay Lydia to defend me at trial.

"I think that's what the DA has in mind," she said. "Grady loses his lawyer. You lose your income. And both of you are looking at jail time. The DA thinks it will help you settle . . . Have you given any more thought," she said carefully, to avoid suggesting what was unethical to suggest, "to how Grady may have come by that chain innocently. If you just had something to take to the jury, anything besides that king-of-Arabia story, none of this would be a problem."

The thing was, I did have something. I had the killer alibi. I just couldn't use it without putting Abby and Shelley in jail.

When I finished explaining what had really happened on the beach the night Grady was supposed to have been digging for treasure, Lydia paused for a few seconds. Then she asked what I should have asked weeks ago. She wanted to know whether Abby and Shelley were the only people who knew what had happened that night.

Of course they weren't. But the drug runners weren't going to testify. They were dead. And, judging from my conversation with the DEA lady, the Feds weren't going to come to my aid, either.

"What about," Lydia asked quietly, "those earthmovers down in Lantern Rock? Think there might be some help from that direction?"

39

THE NEXT MORNING, I set out for Lantern Rock armed with the date October 19, 1971, and no better plan than to try to spot the earth-moving company as I drove by, step inside, introduce myself, and then convince an accessory-after-the-fact to stand up in court and swear he had been taking money to dispose of murdered drug runners.

I was pretty sure there weren't going to be two earthmoving companies in a place like Lantern Rock, and I was right. There was only one, and it had been in the same location since 1946, when the man who'd founded it had come home from the Seabees.

The company had a nice-looking office. It was paneled in some dark kind of wood with big, colorful photographs of heavy equipment on the walls, and a stack of dusty styrofoam cups next to a stainless-steel coffee urn, which, from the taste of the coffee, the new management didn't have much flair for using.

The new management was named Adele. She'd gotten the company two years earlier, at the same time she'd gotten the divorce from the old management. To hear her tell it, she'd gotten fucked, too.

For someone so quick to let you know she was only one jump ahead of food stamps, Adele seemed to be doing pretty well for herself. She wore a nice sweater, had a cute skirt and understated, Egyptian-looking earrings. Judging from the coffee, she was not skilled in domestic matters, and she had definitely been hanging around earthmovers too long, because she had the trashiest mouth I have heard on any human being this side of the United States army. And she was much more interested in her ex-husband than in moving earth.

"He told me he was running a serious business and I believed him.

So when the time came, naturally, I went for the business. And I got it, too, only then I find out he hadn't been running a business at all. He'd been running a toy company."

Adele jerked her finger at the far wall. "That's a brand-mother-fucking-new D7 Cat up there. How the fuck did he come up with something like that on the money this place brings in?" Sure enough, there on the wall next to an enormous elk head was a photograph of a bulldozer.

"Here I am, trying to keep body and soul together practically on cocksucking food stamps"—she stabbed at a picture of her ex-husband looking prosperous next to a bright yellow front-end loader—"and he flushed money on this shit."

The elk head had a little brass plaque announcing:

OCT 18, 1965
LARGEST ELK EVER TAKEN IN MALHEUR COUNTY

"You know about that?" she asked when she calmed down enough to notice where I was looking.

I shook my head.

"Well, everybody in Malheur County sure does, I can tell you that. They're all laughing at me over there, I was such a naïve little cunt." She grimaced at what a naïve little cunt she'd been.

I didn't know what to say to that, so I asked if her ex had shot the elk head.

"Fuck no," she snarled as if the dead elk were all my fault. "He got it at a yard sale in Tillamook."

The Pioneer Museum must have run out of space in the attic.

"He had the plaque made up so I'd think he was out hunting elk all those years instead of pussy. Most years he didn't even have an elk tag. God, was I naïve." She glared at the huge head, as if it were all the elk's fault, too. "I knew you couldn't just go out and buy an elk tag, I knew the Department of Fish and Game holds a lottery every year. And every year Dick Brain heads off for the whole month of

October hunting elk in Malheur County just like he'd won the lottery, and I fell for it hook, line, and sinker."

"October?" I was beginning to have a bad feeling about this. "He went elk hunting in October?"

"Elke hunting. Her name was Elke. For twenty-three goddamn years. Closed the business down and headed off to Malheur County where he had that little . . . Here." She pulled her divorce file out of a drawer, as if she thought I might want to relitigate the property settlement for her. "It's all here. If Elke hadn't been a bookkeeper and Dick Brain hadn't put the makes on her daughter, I never would have found out about it."

"Your ex closed down the earthmoving business every October?" I was having trouble keeping the conversation on point.

"You got that shit right. The little prick took the whole crew with him, just like they'd all won the elk lottery. Cost us a month's income every year. Wanted to improve employee relations, he told me. But that wasn't the kind of relations he was thinking about."

I was definitely getting a bad feeling about this. Malheur County is on the other side of the state, on the Nevada-Idaho border. To get there from Lantern Rock, you have to cross the Coast Range *and* the Cascades and, then, hundreds of miles of lava beds and desert, all on winding, two-lane roads. There was no way Dick Brain could have taken a phone call late at night, then driven back through the lava beds and desert, recrossed the Cascades and the Coast Range, and still arrived at Lantern Rock in time to load a backhoe onto a trailer, truck up to Neahkahnie Beach, bury three dead drug runners, motor back to Lantern Rock, clean the backhoe, and top off the tank with diesel so it wouldn't look as if anything had happened, all before sunup. Unless, it occurred to me, he hadn't really been in Malheur County.

"Did he ever come home for a day or two, then go back?"

"Lick me," she almost spat in her coffee. "He didn't come anywhere except between the legs of that slut bookkeeper. This was Elke season, for fuck's sake. She testified about it for two days at the divorce hearing.

What a joke. She had receipts from motels and gas stations and restaurants straight through the month of October, every year from 1956 through 1978. My lawyer said she'd never seen so much paper. Dick Brain will think twice next time before balling a bookkeeper, I can tell you that."

I was going to have to think twice, too. Whoever had been running a backhoe on Neahkahnie Beach on the night of October 19, 1971, it hadn't been an earthmoving company from Lantern Rock. And without earthmovers to testify for us, our killer alibi was dead.

Usually I enjoy the company of women and invent excuses to be around them. But, in Adele's case, I was out of there as soon as I could get the car started. Besides, I was looking at a long drive to Neahkahnie Mountain, and I wanted to find a decent cup of coffee before I set out.

I had an odd experience on the way. It seemed like the kind of thing that must mean something, only I couldn't see what. I was heading up the Coast Highway trying to figure out how to convince a jury Grady had come by his chain legitimately when I noticed a whale playing in the surf.

It's slow, driving anywhere on the Oregon Coast. Back in the early seventies, the Highway Department thought they would do something about that and drew up plans to expand the highway to four lanes. But the project fell through when the governor pointed out that making it easier to drive along the Oregon Coast would bring more people to the Oregon Coast. Three decades later, the Oregon Coast is still mostly undeveloped, and that same two-lane blacktop is still the only way to get around.

It's a pretty road. Sometimes it curls past little beaches sheltering beneath cliffs, then over fields of weathered lava where waves surge through chambers to spout into geysers thirty or forty feet into the air. Sometimes, big Pacific rollers smash against rocks so close to the road the salt spray blows over your car. Other times, the highway climbs hundreds of feet into misty forests and across rocky streams that fall away in sparkling waterfalls to the ocean below.

I pulled over when I spotted the whale and got out of the car. I'd been trying to see a whale for a long time. Whale-watching is a big deal in Oregon, and I'd seen plenty of spouts, but never a whale. Whales are dark and low in the water and almost invisible from any kind of distance. Over the years, I have met a lot of people who've spotted spouts—but nobody who's ever actually spotted a whale.

And, here one was, in the surf next to the beach, right where kids would be playing if the ocean had been warmer. It loafed along in the unhurried manner of a sleepy tourist taking in the sights. Then, after an indolent half hour, it flipped its flukes and turned lazily out to sea.

There was something unnerving about having spent so much time searching the horizon, only to discover the one whale I ever actually saw, so close by I could have waded out and high-fived it. That something so big could turn out to be so underfoot seemed as if it must mean something. But knowing something must mean something, and knowing what that something means—well, that's something else entirely, and I got back in my car and headed on up to Grady's.

40

NOW THAT OUR killer alibi had died on us, I was back to having to make something out of that crackpot, the-king-of-Arabia-gave-me-the-chain bullshit he'd told the DA. The thing was, I couldn't prove Grady had even been to Saudi Arabia.

Showing where he had been stationed in the army should have been easy, it would have been listed on his discharge papers. But Grady didn't have his discharge papers. "Why would I want to keep that military shit?" He gave me a blank look, as if being the only veteran on the planet who hadn't hung on to his discharge papers made perfect sense.

I contacted the National Archives and Records Administration about it, but they didn't know where he had been stationed, either. Apparently there had been a fire in the cave outside St. Louis where they stored old service records. Their advice was to contact the veteran in question. Veterans, they informed me, always keep copies of their discharge papers.

It wasn't that Grady trod a thin line between sanity and craziness, exactly. The line Grady trod looped through the beating heartland of both kingdoms, and in and out and back again. On a lot of topics, he was more than coherent. He was sharp and insightful and perfectly capable of assisting in his defense. That's the legal standard for being sane enough to stand trial: whether the defendant is capable of assisting in his own defense. But, the closer the trial date came, the less Grady seemed to think he needed defending at all.

"Look here." He pulled the criminal complaint out of the pleadings file. "It's not just the cornerstones of King Solomon's Temple anymore.

This one has ancient-history connotations. Powerful forces are at work. Powerful forces." Grady began to draw igloos across the bottom of the criminal complaint. They looked a lot like the igloos he had drawn on the place mat from the SurfSea, only there were seven this time.

"The Seven Gates of the Underworld," he said softly. "That's what's down there. Ereshkigal, Queen of the Great Below, made Inanna take off her garments outside each gate until she was completely naked." I thought I noticed Grady give a slight bow when he mentioned Inanna's name.

"And jewelry. Her jewelry is down there, too. She had to take off her jewelry along with her clothes. She left that chain for me." He gave me a sly smile. "But that's not the point. As Lord Jesus said, 'The treasures I offer are not of this world.'"

Jesus? How did Jesus . . . ?

"He knew." Grady's beefy face shone with the light of the true believer. "Whoever figured out the secret of Queen Inanna would achieve eternal . . . Look." He stabbed the last igloo with his finger. "Do you have any idea what happened when she passed through the final gate?"

I imagined she had been pretty chilly without her clothes, but I just shook my head. Grady was my best-paying client.

"She passed through the Seventh Gate naked, like Jesus on the cross. But here's the important part," Grady said quietly. "Ereshkigal fixed the Eye of Death on her, and then hung her corpse on the wall."

"So why"—I could not begin to get to the psychosexual bottom of this—"if that Ereshki gal was going to fix the—"

"Ereshkigal," Grady corrected me with quiet dignity, "Queen of the Great Below."

"—if Ereshkigal was going to fix the Eye of Death on her, why did Inanna go down there in the first place?"

"They made her because she was fickle. She took the lion as a lover, and then the stallion. Then, Ishullanu the Gardener, but she turned him into a frog after she gathered in his offerings. Then, Dumuzi the Shepherd. But that's not the point. The point is—"

206

The point is, I thought, I have a genuine crazy man for a client.

"—three days later Enki, the God of Wisdom, fashioned a pair of creatures out of the dirt from under his fingernails and sent them down after her. They made friends with Ereshkigal and did her favors, and in return she took down Inanna's body and gave it to them. When they carried it back to the light, Enki sprinkled it with the food and the waters of life and Inanna arose, reborn. Even the part about the dirt under the fingernails, it all fits. Don't you see?" Grady held out his hands with excitement. "I've got dirt under my fingernails. That's how I knew."

"The dirt under the fingernails?" I looked at Grady. "That was meant for you?"

"Me. You. Anybody. Diggers have dirt under their nails. It's a clue so you know you have to dig. That monk knew. The one who was prisoner on the ship. They were looking for the entrance to the underworld. That's what the carvin's on the rocks are tryin' to tell you, if you know how to read them."

"You know how to read them?"

"I don't speak Sumerian." Grady gave me a look as if I were stupid. "That monk, he was the last one. The language is lost, now. It doesn't make any difference, because nobody ever found the rocks he carved. But you don't have to look at rocks. Look anywhere. All the stories come to the same place. It's right here in Genesis." Grady brushed aside a pistol to get at the Bible on a coffee table.

"Genesis three: twenty-two. 'And the Lord God said, Behold, the man is become as one of us, to know good and evil: and now, lest he put forth his hand, and take also from the tree of life, and eat, and live for ever.' See. Right here. The tree of life."

"The tree of life is under Neahkahnie Mountain?" That *would* be a find.

"Tree of life. Waters of life. Something people have been looking for, for a very long time. Enoch. Jesus. Inanna. Osiris. Dracula. Mohammed. Lazarus. Those who never died. Or came back." Grady leaned closer, as if we were conspirators. "That's why Solomon left those cornerstones from his temple. To mark the place. And Sir Francis Drake. Why do you think Queen Elizabeth locked up the log from his voyage? Because buried at the bottom of Neahkahnie Mountain is the secret of eternal life. That gold chain . . ."

That's when it finally hit me. Grady really had dug it up on Neahkahnie Beach, just as the DA claimed. Only he didn't think it came from a wrecked Spanish ship, anymore. Or, from a secret mission to the king of Arabia, either. By now, he'd convinced himself Queen Inanna had left it for him when she'd passed through the gates of the underworld—which didn't make sense, even in Grady's world.

"That chain," I told him, "is covered with verses from the Koran. It couldn't possibly have come from ancient Sumer."

"The Koran," Grady deflected my objections off the bright shield of his schizophrenia, "was dictated by God."

I nodded.

"Well, don't you get it?" he said. "No earthly goldsmith could have inscribed those verses thousands of years before Mohammed wrote them down. That proves the chain belonged to a goddess." Grady waved the criminal complaint with the igloos at me. "Powerful forces are at work, here. Powerful. That DA doesn't have any idea what he is dealing with."

41

A FEW DAYS before Grady's trial, the Poverty-Law Center, Free Legal Clinic in Garibaldi filed a motion to intervene. According to the motion, the rightful owner of his chain was a thirty-one-year-old Native American named Nelson Coates, who would have inherited it from his grandmother if Grady hadn't stolen it first.

Four years earlier, Nelson Coates had shut down the entire north-Oregon razor-clam industry when he'd announced that the mudflats where the razor clams lived had been granted to his people by President Franklin Pierce in 1855. That the treaty in question had gone all the way to the United States Supreme Court in 1946, only to be rejected, didn't bother Nelson Coates—it was the same government that had stolen the land in the first place that was trying to tell him the treaty wasn't valid.

That his entire tribe had officially ceased to exist in 1954 under the Western Oregon Termination Act bothered him even less. Nelson Coates knew he was an Indian. And, regardless of what the Supreme Court said, he knew those mudflats belonged to his people. And, by the time the Razor-Clam Rebellion was over, half of all razor clams taken along the north-Oregon coast did belong to his people—all fourteen of his people who still identified with the tribe and cared to wade out in the mud to dig for clams. That Nelson Coates was involved was enough, by itself, to bring our case to a complete stop until the matter of who used to own Grady's chain was cleared up. We had a conference in chambers over it.

What Nelson Coates wanted the judge to do or, rather, what the stylishly dressed, severe-looking lawyer he had picked up from New

Jersey by way of the Poverty-Law Center, Free Legal Clinic in Garibaldi wanted the judge to do, was to make the DA withdraw the indictment under the Sunken Treasure Act, then go back to the grand jury and get a new indictment listing Nelson Coates, not the State of Oregon, as the rightful owner of the chain.

Legal hearings can become pretty convoluted, and I have sat through some strange proceedings in my time, but nothing in my memory holds a candle to what went on in chambers that morning. It wasn't just that there was an elephant in the room nobody wanted to talk about, there was a whole circus of elephants dancing on their hind legs in little pink tutus.

In the first place, I shouldn't even have been there. I should have resigned as Grady's lawyer the moment Nelson Coates intervened because, as soon as he did, a Grand Canyon of a conflict had opened up between my interests and his. Not to put too fine a point on it, but I needed the motion to succeed because, once the DA claimed Nelson Coates was the rightful owner of the chain, the Sunken Treasure Act would no longer be part of the case, and the indictment against me for conspiring to fence Grady's chain under the act was out the window. But that's not what Grady needed.

What Grady needed was for the motion to be denied. That trumped-up Grady-must-have-stolen-the-chain-because-he-couldn't-afford-to-own-something-that-nice argument was about as flimsy as you could get. With any luck, it wouldn't make any more sense to a jury than it did to anybody else, and Grady would walk. The last thing he needed was to have the case brought in the name of a real person who'd actually had the chain stolen. Especially when that real person was Nelson Coates.

The problem was, there was no way I could resign without explaining how I'd found out about the indictment against me that created the conflict in the first place. Things were complicated enough without kicking off a criminal investigation into how, exactly, I knew what had gone on inside a grand-jury room. And the DA and the judge couldn't say anything about it until I was arrested, because I wasn't supposed to know about it. So all three of us had to sit stone-faced through the hearing, pretending the huge, snorting indictment dancing around the chambers didn't exist.

Other than that the DA didn't have to worry about going to jail, his position wasn't any better than mine. Since proving the chain had been stolen had always been the weak part of his case, he should have been delighted to have somebody fill the hole for him. But, he didn't want to give up the charges against me because, if that happened, he wouldn't have any way to pressure Grady to turn over the rest of the treasure. So, instead of taking Nelson Coates's side, he tried to persuade the judge that, even though a lawyer representing the real owner was sitting right there in chambers with us, he still wanted to proceed on the basis that Grady couldn't possibly have stolen the chain from anywhere other than state land.

That old judge wasn't exactly a pillar of evenhanded justice, either. He didn't care about saving my butt, at least I don't think he did, he just didn't appreciate being pressured into signing the bullshit warrant for my arrest. Signing warrants was not what he was about, especially against somebody he had right in his chambers and could talk to. Then, when Nelson Coates filed his motion to intervene, the judge realized that all he needed to do to slap the Department of Justice into place, and to get out of having to sign the warrant at the same time, was to grant the motion. And that's how he was going to rule, no matter what arguments the DA made.

For a while, I thought the severe-looking lawyer who represented Nelson Coates was the only one playing it straight, but given the way Grady's case turned out, I'm not even sure of that, anymore. It was hard to tell what her game was. She wasn't skilled at making her arguments, but, what she lacked in subtlety, she made up for with assertiveness. Mostly what she did was wave around an affidavit from one Anna Cook stating that she, Mrs. Cook, had examined the state's photograph of Grady's chain and would positively identify it at trial as the very chain that had been stolen from her sister, Nelson Coates's grandmother.

The DA, who should have been on her side, told the judge that an affidavit wasn't good enough, that he had the right to cross-examine Mrs. Cook to determine whether she could, in fact, positively identify the chain.

The judge, who had already decided that the affidavit was more than good enough to get him where he wanted to go, pointed out that cross-examining witnesses was what trials are for, and—he gestured at me—he was certain the defense would do more than an adequate job of examining all the witnesses when the time came.

I tried to take Grady's side, but my heart wasn't in it. I told the judge not to be so sure, my experience in such matters was limited, and I might not be able to get the truth out of Mrs. Cook.

The judge noted that, as hard as I had worked over the past few months to demonstrate my incompetence, he wasn't sufficiently impressed to change his mind. Then, he stood and walked over to his credenza and poured each of us a whiskey, except the severe-looking lawyer. She was some kind of teetotaler vegetarian who didn't approve of . . . well, it's hard to say all the things she didn't approve of because she had the sense to keep the list to herself, but it was pretty clear she wasn't charmed by the idea of whiskey. Or, from the looks she burned across the room, the chain-saw bear, either.

With the whiskey settling into our systems, the judge explained what he had decided days ago, that he was going to require the DA to withdraw his complaint, go back to the grand jury for a new complaint listing Mr. Coates as the rightful owner, and file the action against Grady all over again.

The DA took one last shot at talking the judge out of it and explained that, regardless of how things looked to other people, it was his case and he wanted to bring it on the grounds that Grady Jackson had stolen the chain from state land. Then he pointed out what he would probably have pointed out at the beginning, if he hadn't been worried about how many Indians would vote for him next election, and told the judge that the court couldn't even entertain Mr. Coates's motion.

He was right about that. Nothing in Oregon law allows a private citizen to intervene in a criminal case, no matter how strongly that private citizen might feel about the case.

The judge never ruled on whether the motion was proper. He didn't have to. He just reminded the DA of what he had been telling him all along, that if he couldn't come up with a better theory than Grady must have stolen the chain because he was too poor to own such a nice thing, then he, the judge, was going to look favorably on a motion for a judgment of acquittal, and the DA wasn't going to have any case at all. And, now that Mr. Coates was prepared to come forward with evidence the chain had really been stolen, the DA would be well advised . . . very well advised . . . to go back to the grand jury and get an indictment listing Nelson Coates as the rightful owner. Then he could bring a case that had a chance of getting to the jury. He should be grateful the court was allowing him to refile his case. When the judge had finished, the DA looked even more sorrowful than usual.

Then, the judge stood and slid into his robe. "Gentlemen"—he nodded at us—"lady. It's time to put it on the record." And, with those words, the case under the Sunken Treasure Act ceased to exist, the DA was forced to withdraw the warrant to have me arrested, and the conflict between my interests and Grady's evaporated as if it had never been. The DA could still charge Grady with stealing the chain from Nelson Coates's grandmother, which he did, but there wasn't any way he could come after me, anymore.

The one, last elephant I didn't see any reason to call attention to during the hearing was that the DA was right. He didn't need Nelson Coates to bring his case. He didn't even need the chain. If he'd just looked a little harder, he could have charged Grady with stealing a whole chestload of treasure from state land. The lady who ran the motel in Manzanita had been watching while Grady lugged it off Neahkahnie Beach—the very night, it turned out, he sent the archaeologist home. She'd told me about it weeks before, when I'd checked in after one of my trips to see Grady.

42

THE MOTEL WAS right across the street from Neahkahnie Beach, and anything that came from the beach belonged to the State of Oregon.

Around the turn of the last century, Governor Oswald West had confiscated the entire coastline, from the Washington border all the way to California, for use as a highway. It was not a well-thought-out idea. The Oregon Coast is not Daytona. Any driver who tried that route would have to curve in and out and back on himself so many times, it would be quicker to swim to California. That's not even counting the collapsing cliffs and mud slides from winter storms, and the Highway Department had better sense than to get involved with a project like that. Seventy years later, the state still hadn't given back the beaches, though, which meant that whatever Grady found out there belonged to it.

By the time I checked into the motel, the whole town knew about his chain, and a lot of people were talking about him. The lady who ran the motel was one of them. She was a regular Grady Jackson groupie. She even had newspaper clippings spread out under the glass next to the cash register.

"I could of told them he found something out there," she said when she noticed where I was looking. She was wearing a shawl that half-concealed a tiny baby clamped to her breast. The shawl was less successful at concealing the breast.

"Now, I'm not one of your people down at the Neahkahnie Club who're always complaining about the digging. I run a motel, so I'm in favor of that kind of thing. Tourists like it, and sometimes it brings them back."

She gave her shawl a careless tug. "I always thought of myself like those storekeepers up in the Gold Rush. Here was Grady Jackson prospecting for the Treasure Houses of Lost Atlantis, or the Golden Hoard of Tamerlane, or whatever other damn thing he was hot on the trail of this week, and I figured I'd be glad for whatever tourist money it threw my way. You from Portland?"

I nodded.

"Figured you for somebody interested in treasure."

"Figured?"

"Sure." She grinned at the mud spattered on my pants from where I had crossed Grady's yard to get to my car. "Looks like you been tramping around trying to decide where to start digging."

"I'm a lawyer." I didn't think I was *that* muddy.

"Never saw a lawyer get himself dirty." She laughed. "You sure you're a lawyer?"

"Pretty sure." I laughed back.

"Well, lawyer or not, don't waste your time. Whatever used to be out there, it ain't there, anymore. Grady Jackson hauled it away ten years ago." The baby made a yawning sound and stretched a tiny arm out from under the shawl. Then, went back to nursing.

"Nobody ever thought he would find anything, and we all made fun of him. Looking back, I'm pretty sure that's the way he wanted it."

"Why," I wondered, "would anybody want to be made fun of?"

"So people wouldn't think he found something. That way he got to keep it. On pretty days, we'd sit on rocks and eat picnic lunches and watch him throw sand out of that hole of his. Some of us would make sandwiches, and other people would bring potato salad, and there would be a lot of laughing and speculating about what he was going to find." Little smacking noises came from under the shawl.

"I was there the day he pulled up the blade from a silver dagger. At least he told everybody it was the blade from a silver dagger. He knew because he couldn't melt it. All I know is, a lot of us thought it was part of an old furnace. But none of that cut any mustard. The dagger was pointing the way the rocks said it was supposed to point, and that was good enough for Grady."

She unplugged the baby and switched it to the other side. "He talked a lot about this L-shaped marlinespike he found. He claimed they always bent marlinespikes into *L*'s to mark the Lord's Treasure. So, whatever was buried down there must have been buried in English. Next thing, he started saying that the *L* was for *Elohim*, which is the Jewish word for 'Lord.' So, the treasure was actually buried in Hebrew, which proved it was the Queen of Sheba's gold he was on the track of." The baby wriggled and let go with a loud burp. Then turned and stretched, again, as the erect, wet nipple bobbed gently beside its ear.

I was embarrassed to be staring, but the motel lady didn't seem to notice. She pulled the shawl across her breast in a lazy motion, then slid a registration form in my direction. Something about her standing loose-jointed and relaxed with her baby made me like her.

"Then Grady remembered that *L* is the Roman number for fifty. 'Well, don't you get it?' he'd say. 'They left that marlinespike to let me know I was only fifty cubits from the treasure. So all I have to do is measure off fifty cubits, and I'll have it.'" She turned languidly and waved through a side door into another room.

"I love my kids dearly, it's just with my Harold off driving that truck all the time, I do miss talking to grown-ups. And you seemed like . . ."

"No." I leaned against the counter. "Please go on."

She adjusted the shawl. "The thing was, that backhoe bothered one of the guests so much . . ." A blond head, then another head, poked through the door. "Mom," the younger, blonder head demanded, "when are we going to eat?"

"Just let me get this gentleman situated." She turned back to me. "Down to the left and up the stairs. Room 206." She dropped a key onto the counter.

"Usually it's pretty quiet out here, but, that night, a car had been backfiring. Then Grady cranked up that backhoe of his, and this one old fellow who had driven all the way from Kansas for his second honeymoon kept calling to complain about the noise. I figured the real noise he wanted me to do something about was right there in the room with him. His wife had been calling him a cheapskate for staying here in the first place, and it must have been hell having to listen to her complaining about the backhoe." A sleepy eye looked out from under the shawl and shut pleasantly.

"Anyway, about two in the morning, instead of just leaving the phone off the hook, I grabbed my coat and went outside to see if I could get Grady to tone it down. I knew it was Grady because that turtle-green Chevy of his was parked about four hundred yards down the beach. There was no mistaking that car. But, before I could get across the street, the backhoe stopped." The baby wriggled and stretched out a tiny arm and turned toward the nipple. And went back to sleep.

"I was about to come inside when something caught my eye coming toward the car. There was just enough light to make out Grady staggering across the beach with something big and square in his arms. Now, Grady Jackson is pretty big, himself, but he had trouble with that chest, and when he set it down, it fell apart, it was so old and rotten, and he had to scoop it up in handfuls to get it in his trunk. He took a long time doing it, and when I went out there the next day, I couldn't find any pieces of it, so he was pretty thorough.

"He must have left some treasure behind so he could handle the chest, or there was more in that hole of his, because when he finished loading the first pile in the trunk, he took a garbage bag out on the beach for the rest." She pulled the shawl tighter around her narrow shoulders.

"Next morning, when the old fellow checked out, he thought I was responsible for shutting Grady up, and he left me a hundred-dollar gift certificate to the sporting-goods store he ran in Topeka, which I had no way of using, so his wife was right about him being a cheapskate. Coffee in the morning?"

I nodded.

"Pot'll be ready by six."

43

BACK AT THE office, I had an appointment with a gentleman from the bar. He'd come for the blackmail tapes and shredded cash we'd found at Thaddeus's Secret Love Nest.

Strictly speaking, I wasn't sure I'd had to tell the bar about those things. The court order they'd dropped off the morning Thaddeus had died hadn't said anything about any cabins at Zigzag Creek, it just required us to turn over whatever was in the office. So I had grounds to argue that what we'd shot out of the safe wasn't covered.

On the other hand, I'd been there when we'd shot them out. Looked at unkindly, you could even make the case I had been in charge of the shooting. At the least, I was involved up to my eyeballs, and I couldn't help thinking the safest thing was to get rid of the cash and tapes before somebody decided I was trying to steal them. So I called the bar and mentioned that a few more items had shown up, and to please come take them away.

I guess what had already come out of Thaddeus's office was spooky enough that suddenly discovering a pile of bullet-shredded twenties and a cigar box filled with blackmail tapes that had somehow been missed by all three searches didn't raise any eyebrows. Whatever. Nobody asked where they'd come from, and it wasn't my job to answer questions that weren't asked. My job was to get rid of what we found before I got caught.

"Twenty-eight microcassettes," Jolene said, smiling sweetly as she handed the cigar box to the man from the bar.

It took a moment to realize what bothered me about that. There had been twenty-nine tapes in that box the night we shot open the safe. I was almost certain.

But not certain enough to make an issue out of it. I could see where something like that would lead. The moment I told the investigator there might once have been twenty-nine, he was going to want to know where the twenty-ninth tape was. Then he was going to want to know, where had the tapes come from in the first place? So I made a quick mathematical calculation and decided that twenty-eight was within 3 or 4 percent of twenty-nine, and that the extra tape—even if there had been an extra tape—was lost in the margin of error.

Once the investigator was safely on his way, I took a close look at the inventory sheet. The 28 had been written with a ballpoint pen. The 8 seemed awkward and tilted to the right. And the bottom loop was a little straighter than it should have been, as if somebody had changed it from a 9. The loop was also in black ink, while the rest of the 8 was blue.

"That's easy," Jolene explained, innocent as a plum when I asked who had changed the number. "I did. We only gave the bar twenty-eight tapes and I wasn't going to lie about something as important as that."

She crossed her arms with the satisfied air of somebody who had seen her duty and done it. "Shelley took one home with him the night we got back from the Love Nest. He didn't steal it, don't get me wrong. Abby was one of your best clients, and when he asked me nicely if he could please have the tape, I told him sure. I knew you wanted to keep her happy." And that, as far as Jolene was concerned, was that.

The part I couldn't figure was what Shelley wanted with the tape. Thaddeus wouldn't have had anything on him. He hadn't known Shelley. And it was hard to see why anybody would need a tape to blackmail Abby. While Thaddeus was alive, the only thing she'd cared about had been her stash, and if he'd known about that, he wouldn't have needed a tape at all. All he'd have to do was threaten to call the sheriff.

I was right about the blackmail part, too. I listened to enough of the tapes to make sure of that. Then, when I'd come across a conversation between Thaddeus and a judge out in Oregon City, I'd shut off the machine. There were some things in that cigar box I was better off not knowing.

For months after the bar took the tapes, I expected to read about that judge in the paper. Or, at least, hear stories from other lawyers, but I never did. The Oregon bar is famous for circling the wagons, so they may just have circled around that judge. Still, what went on between him and Thaddeus was pretty hot stuff, and I was surprised nothing ever came of it.

What was on the tapes I never listened to, I have no idea. To this day, every time a likely candidate doesn't run for office, or some legislator makes an unexpected political compromise, or somebody important suddenly resigns from something, I think about those tapes and wonder whether they are still around and try to remember the names on the labels. Sometimes, I'm pretty sure I recognize some. But, who knows? Candidates decide not to run, and politicians compromise, and people resign from office every day for perfectly good reasons they don't tell me about.

44

SELECTING JURORS FOR Grady's trial wasn't as easy as it had been for Abby's. With Abby, I had wanted ne'er-do-wells and the trainee DA had wanted solid citizens. With Grady, I wasn't so sure what I wanted. Half the people in Siletz County had visited his bar at one time or another, and the other half knew all about the Crazy Man of Neahkahnie Mountain. I couldn't figure out whether that helped or hurt, so I just asked the people on the panel whether they approved of gun control, and whether they took the Bible literally.

The Sorrowful DA asked the jurors whether they had any connection with the razor-clam industry, and if they did, he struck them from the panel. He wasn't worried about what people thought of Grady, he was worried what they thought of Nelson Coates. That deputy in the hallway had been right. The Sorrowful DA did know the people down there better than I did.

When we were finished challenging jurors, we had a logger on the jury, a sharpener from a sawmill, two housewives, and a lady who chopped the heads off fish in a cannery. We would have had a waitress from a restaurant that specialized in razor clams, but the Sorrowful DA struck her in favor of a blind dentist who had tried to get out of jury duty on the grounds that he couldn't afford the time off from work. The old judge didn't buy it, though, and we wound up with the dentist, too.

The logger and the saw-sharpener and the lady who chopped heads off fish were gun owners, and I made a point of emphasizing Grady's home-decorating scheme in my opening statement. Those three also struck me as people who might like to take a drink, so I played up the bartender angle as well, but I couldn't tell how any of it went over. The housewives and the blind dentist were complete blanks.

When the trial started, Nelson Coates, a state trooper, and a demure, white-haired lady who could only have been Anna Cook were waiting in the back of the courtroom. I'd taken depositions of Nelson Coates and the trooper, but I didn't have any idea what Mrs. Cook was going to say. When I'd tried to meet with her, she refused. I thought about subpoenaing her, but Grady told me to leave her be. "I know the Cooks," he said. "They are the closemouthedest people in the world, even with each other. And you're white."

Ordinarily, the first witness would have been the state trooper. The Sorrowful DA would have used him to set the scene by telling the jury he'd found the gold chain at Grady's house. But that morning, Mr. Coates had to leave for an important activist conference, so the DA called him first.

Nelson Coates was tall and dignified, and he looked exactly the way a young Indian activist from the early eighties was supposed to look. He was wearing a split-leather, suede jacket, a silver-and-turquoise watchband that matched his silver-and-turquoise belt buckle, and what were almost certainly highly illegal endangered-eagle feathers tied with leather strips into the long braids over his shoulders. Nobody in authority, I was sure, was ever going to make an issue out of those feathers. In some important ways, Nelson Coates had won just by dressing for court. That he dressed like a Plains Indian, rather than somebody from the Oregon Coast, didn't seem to bother anybody.

Nelson Coates told the jury how he had been an idealistic teenager growing up in Garibaldi, how he liked cowboy movies, how he had volunteered to fight in Vietnam, and how, when he'd seen what our army was doing over there, he had come to understand that our government, even with the best of intentions, sometimes betrays and victimizes other peoples. Then, while he was at Madigan General Hospital recovering from the wound to his leg and, just incidentally, costing Grady whatever war-hero sympathy I might have been able to drum up, his grandmother had told him how the very same government he had fought for, had reneged on the treaty that had guaranteed his people the right to hunt and fish over their traditional hunting and fishing grounds.

There was no way to cross-examine that, and I just let him go. It wasn't until he had left the courtroom that I realized he hadn't said much. He hadn't even identified the chain. All he'd said was that he remembered that his grandmother had once owned a heavy gold chain that had been handed down in her family for generations. And that the chain had been stolen from her.

But that didn't mean that his testimony wasn't a big hit. Nelson Coates had been so low-key and so convincing and so nonthreatening and filled with brotherly love, I don't think it would have made any difference if a few razor-clam people had slipped onto the jury. By the time he strode, head high in pride from the courtroom, all six jurors were filled with remorse and shame at what our people had done to the rightful inhabitants of this land, which nobody could even begin to make up for, but which we, right here in this courtroom, had the opportunity to put a down payment on by seeing to it that Grady Jackson was punished for stealing their poor, pitiful gold chain. The whole thing had been irrelevant and underhanded and effective. It would send Grady Jackson to jail, and I hadn't been able to do a damn thing to stop it.

It was pretty clear what was coming next. The state trooper was going to tell the jury he had found the chain in Grady's house. Then the demure, white-haired lady in back was going to identify it as the same chain that had been stolen from her sister, and, the DA hoped, Grady Jackson would be off to jail for a long time. Against that, I had Grady as my one, lone witness. If I called him.

Most criminal defendants never testify. The prosecutor can't make them because the Fifth Amendment won't force anybody to testify against himself. And the defense lawyer better think twice before putting his client on the stand. Once he's up there, the prosecutor can ask pretty much anything he wants. So, a criminal defendant who testifies in his own defense had better have something really good to say, or he better just keep sitting at the defense table. Unfortunately, I couldn't even get that cock-and-bull the-king-of-Arabia-gave-me-the-chain story into the record unless Grady told it, and without that story, Grady didn't have any defense at all.

But, with Grady telling the story, there wasn't just the risk of what the DA might ask on cross, there was the danger that Queen Inanna was going to get dragged into the proceedings, and once he finished enlightening the jury on how she had stripped in front of the Seven Gates only to have her naked corpse nailed on the wall, he'd be lucky if he wasn't put away in a special prison for people with scary sexual fantasies. But if I didn't let him testify, I'd concede the trial and he would go straight to ordinary prison.

The DA played it pretty much as I expected. When the trooper got through making sure the jury understood that the chain in question had been found at Grady's, the DA called Mrs. Anna Cook to the stand to explain that it was the same chain that had been stolen from her sister. And, all of a sudden, I didn't need to make a decision about whether to have Grady testify, because Mrs. Cook refused to identify the chain.

She was thoughtful about refusing. She turned the chain in her hand. She held it to the light.

She let it slither from palm to palm.

She placed it against her cheek to feel the coolness of the gold.

She smelled it.

She bit it.

And, when she was satisfied she knew what she had in her hand, she told the DA, "Not chain."

The DA stopped looking sorrowful and started looking flabber-gasted. "Mrs. Cook," he said gently. You have to seem gentle when you question children and old people. If the jury thinks you're a bully, you blow your whole case. "Do you remember when we spoke last week?"

She nodded.

"And, do you remember that I showed you a picture of this chain?"

She nodded, again.

"You will have to answer out loud." The old judge leaned toward Mrs. Cook. "So the court reporter can get what you say into the record."

She nodded politely to the judge.

"And, do you remember that you told me that the chain in the picture, this very chain, was the one that was stolen from your sister?"

Mrs. Cook nodded again and, before the judge could correct her, broke into the longest piece of sustained prose she spoke all morning. "Chain in picture look like chain."

She thought some more about what needed to be added. Then: "This not chain." And, that was that. With one eloquent sentence and two sentence fragments, Anna Cook completely destroyed the case against Grady Jackson.

The DA tried to get her to elaborate, to say anything besides "Not chain," but it was no use. She just sat there nodding and looking very old and very demure and very certain of herself. In the end she stepped down, having never spoken another word on the witness stand.

Maybe Nelson Coates could have saved the day. Maybe he could have climbed back onto the stand and told the jury in his low-key, nonthreatening way that the chain the troopers had found at Grady's was the very chain that had been stolen from his grandmother. But, Nelson Coates was halfway to Portland International Airport on important activist business by then and never got the chance. So, all the DA could do was rest his case.

Instead of calling Grady to the stand, I moved for a judgment of acquittal. I would have moved for that, anyway. Defense lawyers always move for a judgment of acquittal when the prosecution rests. No matter how strong and how detailed the case you just listened to, you stand up, put on your straightest face, and ask the judge to acquit your client on the grounds that the prosecution hasn't even put on enough evidence to allow the case to go to the jury. The judge always denies the motion, and then you call your first witness and get on with the business of showing the defense's side of things.

But not this time.

This time, the judge granted the motion.

The Sorrowful DA tried to argue that it didn't really make any difference who Grady had stolen the chain from. That he had it for any reason proved he had stolen it.

The judge reminded the DA that the charges specifically stated that the chain had, in fact, been stolen from a Molly Coates. And, now that it turned out that the chain had not been stolen from Molly Coates, he had failed to prove his case.

The Sorrowful DA pointed out that if he had been allowed to bring the case the way he had wanted, Grady would be on trial for stealing the chain from state land and Molly Coates wouldn't have anything to do with it.

The judge told the Sorrowful DA that if he still believed the chain had been stolen from state land, he was free to go back to the grand jury and get the original indictment issued all over again. But that he had better think twice before doing so.

Then, the old judge leaned forward and spoke clearly, as if he wanted to make sure the court reporter got each word exactly as he said them, and told the DA that his whole case had been a shambles. That he had brought a good man, and a war hero, to trial on charges that were so thin he hadn't even managed to come up with a single witness to support his wild accusations. At that point, the judge stopped and looked at Grady and said, "I apologize to you, sir, for my part in this travesty."

Then, the judge turned back to the DA and told him he had a good mind to hold him in contempt for wasting the court's time with such nonsense, and that if he dared refile under the Sunken Treasure Act, he would not only dismiss the case out of hand for violating the Fifth Amendment's provision against double jeopardy, he would bring the contempt charges.

The judge gaveled his gavel, and a pair of housewives, a guy who sharpened saws in a sawmill, a logger, a woman who chopped the heads off fish, and a blind dentist went home without ever hearing our side of the story. And Grady walked out of the courtroom a free, if unbalanced, man.

Unfortunately, we were so glad to get out of there I forgot to ask the judge to make the county give back the chain.

45

THE DA CLAIMED he was holding it as evidence. But, as time passed and he never filed any more charges against Grady, I began asking louder and more pointed questions about evidence of what? In the end, we had a hearing over it and the same informal, no-nonsense judge poured each of us a shot of whiskey, then wanted to know the same thing I wanted to know: What did the DA think the chain was evidence of?

The DA gave him a sorrowful look and explained that the chain was evidence of a violation of the Sunken Treasure Act.

The judge smiled in a relaxed sort of way and told the DA that, if he really believed the chain had been stolen from state land, he had sixty days to seek a third indictment from the grand jury and bring charges against Grady on those grounds—if he dared. Or return the chain.

The judge stood, the hearing was over, and we all trooped into the courtroom to put it on the record.

Forty-seven days later, the DA called. He told me that if Grady turned over all the stolen artifacts he had, and I turned over the ones I had, the county would forget about filing the new indictment.

Usually you are supposed to run this kind of thing by your client, but I already knew what my client would say. It was the same deal the DOJ lady had offered months before to keep him out of jail. He had turned it down then. Now that he had won the trial, and the judge was threatening the DA with contempt the moment he brought new charges, Grady didn't have any reason to deal at all.

And there was one more thing. 42 United States Code 1981.

Deprivation of Constitutional Rights under the Color of State Authority. Congress passed it during Reconstruction to stop Southern officials from mistreating newly freed slaves under the pretext of carrying out some local ordinance or other. It was one of the great civil rights statutes of the nineteenth century, but you don't have to be African-American to sue under it. You just have to have had your constitutional rights violated by somebody acting under the color of law. And, if the Sorrowful DA filed charges against Grady again, he would be that somebody. And the constitutional right he would be violating would be Grady's right not to be tried twice for the same crime. At least, that's what I told him.

I had no idea whether it would work in real life, but I had already been tinkering with a formal complaint to see what I could get on paper. By the time the DA called, I had enough on paper to overnight him a copy. I don't know whether he bought the threat, or whether he had been bluffing all along, but he never filed any more charges.

It didn't get the chain back, but Grady liked the idea of threatening the DA so much that, the next time we met, he pulled a roll of twenties out of his shirt pocket and peeled off a bonus for me. It was like that the whole time I worked for him. He paid me in full, in cash, in twenties, all Series 1970 and earlier, just like the twenties in both of Thaddeus's safes. I never had any trouble passing them. They weren't counterfeit and they weren't marked, and apparently there wasn't any record of their serial numbers anywhere. At least nobody ever came around asking me where I got them. Wherever Thaddeus had been fencing Grady's treasure, he had known what he was doing.

On the fifty-third day, the DA called again. He told me that certain high officials were going to intervene in the case unless Grady stopped asking for the chain back.

That afternoon, I filed a third, formal letter to the county demanding the chain.

On the fifty-eighth day, just as the DA promised, high officials intervened in the case. The Department of Justice filed a motion for restitution, claiming Grady had stolen the chain from state land, and asked the judge to declare the chain the property of the State of Oregon.

It was a slick move because it got around the whole question of double jeopardy. Grady wasn't accused of anything. All the state was asking the judge to do was to declare that the chain belonged to them, and since the DA wasn't involved, there wasn't anybody for the judge to hold in contempt. We had a full evidentiary hearing over it.

The only difference between a full evidentiary hearing and a trial is that they call it a hearing, and you don't get to have a jury. Otherwise, it's a trial.

Since this wasn't a criminal proceeding, the state didn't have to show me their evidence beforehand, and as the date approached, I began worrying about the motel lady. She was the person I most did not want to meet in the courtroom. But, the morning of the trial, she wasn't there.

The lawyer for the DOJ called his first witness, who turned out to be some kind of gold-chain expert, who told the judge that, yes, indeed, the gold chain was a gold chain. And that it was in a style consistent with sixteenth-century Middle Eastern workmanship and had most likely been made in Damascus between 1545 and 1573. While he was rambling on, I heard the door open in back, and somebody slipped softly into the courtroom. Then I heard a baby cry and I was sure it was Motel Lady. But, when I turned around, it was just a young mother who had wandered into the wrong room.

The state's next witness was a celebrity metallurgist, if you believed his credentials. He had conducted a nondestructive, spectrographic analysis of the metal in the chain and concluded it was consistent with gold mined in Upper Egypt between the middle seventh century and the early tenth century and was typical of the gold reworked into jewelry in Syria during the 1500s.

Then the state called an expert in Filipino trade during the colonial period. He testified that the chain was just the sort of chain that could have found its way down the Red Sea to India, then to Manila, where it might have been sold to Spanish merchants for loading onto a galleon for the long, dangerous journey to Acapulco, which, often, went right by Neahkahnie Mountain.

It was all very impressive in a mumbo-jumbo, pretend-science sort of way, but all the state had proved was that Grady's chain might have been manufactured in Syria from gold that could have been mined in Upper Egypt, then may have been traded to Manila, where it could have been loaded onto a galleon nobody could name, which might have sailed past Neahkahnie Mountain sometime in the distant past.

If this had been a criminal trial, the judge would have ended the proceedings right there for failure to prove the elements of a crime beyond a reasonable doubt. But this wasn't a criminal trial, it was a civil proceeding, and all the state had to show was that it was more likely than not that the chain had been stolen from state land. And, they had at least shown how it could have wound up on state land.

So, we had to put on a case of our own, and Grady Jackson finally got to tell the judge about King Abdul Aziz ibn Saud and the secret mission to Saudi Arabia. I was proud of him. He didn't say anything about Queen Inanna or Dumuzi the Shepherd Consort, and when the judge asked him if he had any documentation, any photographs or papers, or any witnesses who had actually seen him bring the chain into the country, Grady just answered politely that, under the circumstances, he didn't have any documentation, but he was sure the judge would understand. He did not mention his sister in Tucson.

As an explanation, that king-of-Arabia fantasy was no more bull-shit than what the state had come up with. And it fit the testimony from their chain expert and their celebrity metallurgist just as well as the Manila-galleon theory. Better, I thought, because it was simpler and didn't involve any unidentified sunken ships.

The lawyer for the DOJ must have thought so, too, because, once Grady sat down and I didn't call any other witnesses, he launched into his closing statement—and badly overplayed his hand. He scoffed at the whole idea that Grady even knew the king of Arabia. Then he cranked up the old turkey about how he must have stolen the chain, because he wasn't the kind of person who could have owned it legitimately.

That bullshit some-people-are-too-poor-to-deserve-nice-things was the kind of argument that would have killed him in front of a jury, but, as it turned out, we didn't need a jury. The judge was offended, too. He gave the lawyer for the DOJ a little lecture about how the county had tried to base their first indictment on just that argument, and how he'd told them he would dismiss the claim on the spot if they were rash enough go to trial on such tomfool nonsense. I wasn't exactly sure that's what he'd said to the Sorrowful DA that morning in chambers, but I wasn't going to correct him.

Then he told the state that the only evidence of theft he could see was that the chain had been stolen from Grady and ordered everybody concerned to immediately return it.

And, they still didn't. The DOJ claimed it was going to file some kind of appeal, but the appeal period came and went and nothing happened.

Late summer turned into fall, and the rains started, and the county still hung on to the chain.

Fall turned into the second week of November and, still, no chain. I had to file a motion to find the county in contempt of court, which required scheduling a whole new hearing. It wasn't until the morning of the hearing, five *minutes* before the judge was going to meet us in chambers and, I was sure, pour each of us a shot of whiskey, then find the county and the Sorrowful DA in contempt, that Grady finally got his chain back.

Four days later, he was dead.

46

THE MAILMAN FOUND him on the porch, holding a brochure of Polynesia in his hand. The brochure was from an expensive cruise line.

Three days later, he was still dead. Inanna, Queen of Heaven and fickle as always about the sacrifices of others, did not come back for him. Instead, the Veterans Administration brought him to Portland and buried him in the Willamette National Cemetery in Section N, facing west on the gentle slope of an extinct volcano.

It was a drizzly day in November. Little granite headstones were set ground-level in long rows curving beneath the autumn reds of the oak trees. Bright yellow maples were sprinkled across the hill, too, along with the dark, wet greens of cedars. Everywhere, the cemetery was graceful and reflective and quiet.

Everywhere, except at the graveside.

At the graveside, the hill was scraped down to bare, yellow ground and was messy with heaps of new dirt. Excavation equipment waited in the rain next to half a dozen open graves. Being buried there was like being buried at a construction site. The place they had for Grady was next to a backhoe. Somehow, that seemed fitting.

The service was in a shabby little government pavilion a hundred yards from the grave. The pavilion was open in the front and made of corrugated fiberglass that had crazed and yellowed from too many years in the weather. If Grady's coffin had been set up in a bus shelter, the bus shelter would have seemed comfortable and well-appointed in comparison.

A few army buddies and a lot of people from over on the Coast came to tell him good-bye. No one from his family was there to accept the flag, though, and I felt bad I hadn't thought to call his sister.

Grady went to the hereafter with an eighteen-gun salute and the slowest, most heartrending version of taps I ever heard. As the last, mournful notes faded away, the skies opened, and four fighter jets from the Oregon Air National Guard roared over in the missing-man formation. As the holder of the Distinguished Service Cross, Grady Jackson rated a funeral deluxe. Then the skies really did open up and the drizzle turned into a hard, blowing rain. I figured Grady would have liked that.

There wasn't any religious person present. For a guy who had so many Bibles lying around his house, nobody seemed to think Grady wanted religion intruding on his death. In the end, a tall, stooped buddy from Guadalcanal spoke. He didn't say a lot, just a few things about how much they all owed to Grady, then wound up with "Edray Eamtay Andedlay."

And the three other buddies from the Pacific picked it up like a benediction: "Edray Eamtay Andedlay."

Pig latin for "Red Team Landed." They were the first words Grady had broadcast after he'd washed up on Guadalcanal. That's when I finally got the inside story about what he had done to earn his Distinguished Service Cross.

I had a little trouble with that Edray Eamtay Andedlay later on. Uncle has pages of National Cemetery Administration Regulations setting out exactly what can go on a marker in a United States cemetery, and Edray Eamtay Andedlay is not on the list. But, being Grady's lawyer, I was anointed by his buddies to make it happen.

The government allows your name on a marker, along with your rank, branch of service, state, date of birth, and date of death. You also get to have an "approved religious emblem" at no extra cost. And a couple of lines on the bottom for endearments or other phrases in good taste, professional titles, or military awards, which, in anybody's case but Grady's, would have included Distinguished Service Cross.

Only, Grady hadn't wanted any of that military shit on his tombstone. So we forgot about the DSC.

Forgetting about rank was a little harder. Everybody gets their rank on their tombstone in a VA graveyard. But, when I parsed the language, the only thing the guidelines said was "regulations allow for the inscription on the marker to be the highest rank achieved by the veteran." When you argue that long enough, it begins to sound a lot like the whole business of rank is optional. Anyway, I pulled it off.

The approved religious emblem was no problem. Not that Grady would have wanted a religious emblem any more than he wanted that military shit, but he got one anyway. When I checked the list of approved emblems, I found some that looked a lot like markings that had been carved into the chunks of beeswax on Neahkahnie Beach. In the end, I settled on a cross with a circle around it. It was also, I discovered later, the Sumerian representation of the sun. They used it with figures of Queen Inanna. Go figure.

It was the Edray Eamtay Andedlay that gave me fits. It's hard to get people as dignified as federal graveyard bureaucrats to admit that pig latin on one of their markers could be in good taste. But Grady's buddies were pretty clear about wanting that exact phrase. "Where Sergeant Grady Jackson is now, he is definitely in enemy territory," his tall, stooped buddy had told me, "and he needs to make it back to friendly lines." The other buddies amen-ed to that. I figured they knew where Grady had gone as well as anybody could know, and I made a point of getting that phrase on his marker. In the end, I claimed it was a term of endearment in Guadalcanalese, and the graveyard people went along.

I checked a few months later, and the cemetery had put it in the ground. So, if you want to see pig latin on a federal grave marker, you can go to Section N, Willamette National Cemetery, and read some for yourself.

After the flyover, the honor guard broke ranks and put on ponchos and straggled off into the rain. The bugler packed up his bugle and left, and the people from the Coast drifted away in ones and twos until it was just the army buddies and me and Grady under the corrugated plastic roof.

"I have something to say," one of the army buddies announced once we were alone. "And it's not going to be in pig latin."

He was dark-haired and broad-shouldered. He had a huge nose and hairy hands and didn't care much one way or another about pig latin because he had never been anywhere near Guadalcanal. "Grady Jackson was the finest engineer soldier I ever met, and I was proud to serve with him."

Then he reached into a grocery bag and pulled out a goblet and a bottle of Kentucky bourbon and poured a toast. As a drinking vessel, the goblet wasn't all that big. But it was pure gold. And it had huge, red stones set around the middle of the bowl that looked an awful lot like uncut rubies to me.

He passed the goblet around, and we each had a swallow in honor of Grady. When the goblet came back, he poured a sip onto the coffin, then passed it around, again.

We had a warm, funny, sad, sentimental good-bye party to the sound of rain thrumming on corrugated plastic. Those old guys lifted the goblet to their buddies who weren't there, and to their buddies who were, and to Grady, but mostly they lifted it to the men they had been in their own, bright youths, long ago. And, every time the goblet came around, Grady had his own, full measure poured onto his coffin. It was the kind of situation that can lead to philosophy if you aren't careful.

"This whole organized-religion thing doesn't make any sense, if you ask me," Grady's dark-haired buddy said slowly. "Any outfit that encourages you to have all those extra wives, that's a situation where a man's just naturally going to need a drink. This cup"—he turned the goblet reflectively in his hand—"I don't think whoever made this cup expected anybody was ever going to drink whiskey out of it."

"You mean that goblet"—I was beginning to put two and two together—"was made by . . . Mormons?" It was easy to imagine it as some kind of sacred chalice that had been lifted from the seventh-floor sanctuary of the Temple in Salt Lake City.

"Mormons?" He gave me a puzzled look. "The king of Saudi Arabia gave it to me. King Abdul Aziz ibn Saud, himself, upon completion of my tour of duty as a guest in his country. And, not just me. We all got something." He laughed at the memory. "Lopez got a sword belt. Grady got a gold chain, and Melderis got a scimitar, but Uncle took it away the moment he stepped on the plane. I don't know what the other guys got, because they shipped home after us. But I can tell you this, wasn't any of it documented. The moment Uncle got wind of anything like that, he was all over it like a pig on turnips." He took a long pull from the goblet.

"You have to understand, we were the first American soldiers ever to go to Saudi. There were just five of us, one squad of engineering soldiers to help train their troops. It wasn't a secret mission, not in the way top-secrets are secret. But it was secret in the confidential sense that it wasn't anything any of us were supposed to talk too much about. The Saudis didn't need the home folks getting upset about infidel troops on their soil.

"Whatever else you say about those people, hospitality is high on their list. When it came time for us to ship home, the king sent around a limousine to bring us to the palace so he could thank us in person. This was in 1951 and there wasn't even a paved road in that country except this one stretch from the palace to the airport." He smiled at the memory.

"When we pulled up to the palace, the king invited us inside. He was wearing these beautiful, black robes with white trim, like he was some kind of fancy holy man or something, only a lot more dignified. He invited us inside and thanked us for all our services to the Kingdom and his family and said he wanted to give us something to remember them by. When he was done thanking us, he had a servant lead us through a whole series of rooms all covered with tiles and paved in marble until we came to this closed door guarded by two huge guys with curved swords, just like eunuchs in the movies.

"All the treasures of Ali Baba and the Forty Thieves were in that room, and this goblet was the least of it. They had gold daggers and

241

curved swords and jeweled boxes; there was a pair of saddles encrusted with pearls, and loose jewels, half of it going back to the time of the Prophet, and the servant invited each of us to choose something for ourselves.

"Well, that took some choosing. The way I figured it, get anything gaudy and Uncle was going to take it away the moment I set foot on that Air Force C-123. Melderis was the only one to make that mistake. But something modest, something like a plain, little goblet, might just slip by. And, it did, too. I mixed it up with some junk I'd picked up at the bazaar and told them I'd paid nine dollars and fifty cents for it, and they laughed and told me I'd been robbed." He grinned and took another long sip. And, then, passed the goblet to me.

I took a long sip, even though it was bourbon. Grady had been telling the truth about the chain. Who would have guessed? But, if it really was from the king of Arabia, then what had Thaddeus been fencing in exchange for the twenties? For that matter, where had the brooch and the rest of the jewelry in his safe come from? Unless . . .

"Is there any way Grady . . . any of you guys"—I was fishing for a polite way to phrase this—"could have walked out of that room with more than just one gift?"

"Are you kidding?" Grady's buddy from his Saudi Arabia days fixed me with a stare as if I were stupid. "That was King Abdul Aziz we were messing with, there. You know what the punishment in Arabia is for stealing?" He held up his hands. "I've still got both mine, thank you very much. There was no way . . . no way any of us would try a stunt like that. Besides, you should have seen the size of those guys guarding the door." He shook his head in amusement. "All the treasures of Araby were in that room. You should have seen that place."

After a while the rain let up, and we finished the bourbon, and it was time to go. I drove back to the office, and Grady's buddies headed over to Neahkahnie Mountain for a private ceremony. I felt sad, leaving Grady alone in his coffin under that fiberglass shelter like that, but the actual burial was something Uncle took care of on his own schedule.

47

HERE'S THE OFFICIAL, oral-history version of what Grady did to earn his Distinguished Service Cross, as told by one of the men who had been with him on Guadalcanal:

"Well, not exactly with Grady, but I was there. I was just getting ready to go outside the wire and relieve the forward listening post, when he comes strolling out of the jungle talking pig latin. They gave him the Distinguished Service Cross for it, only it took from December '42 when he earned it, until April of '45 before the army finally decided that, whatever it was Grady Jackson actually had in mind, he really had saved himself and all eight men in his squad, so they might as well go on and give him the medal.

"The Japs had torpedoed his troopship off the Solomons. There was a lot of that going around, then. Grady and those other eight guys made it into a raft and spent a night and a day and part of the next night drifting this way and that in the tropical sun and jumping into the water and turning the raft upside down so the gray side was up whenever Jap planes flew over.

"They were hungry and thirsty and sunburned to beat all hell when they finally washed up on the shore of Guadalcanal. Unfortunately for them, they washed up on the shore where the Japs were. The Japs knew they were there, too, because a Betty came in on a strafing run just as they were pulling across the reef, which was bad luck for them because Bettys didn't fly at night. But there one was, and the moon was out and the raft was leaving this phosphorescent trail across the water and wouldn't have been easier to spot if they'd just drawn a line to it on a map. That Betty must have been on the way home from

243

patrol because it only fired a couple of tracers and then it flew off like it had run out of bullets. The pilot wasn't out of radio waves, though, and nobody had any doubt who'd be waiting for them once they got onshore.

"Now, anybody but Grady Jackson would have put as much distance between himself and that beach as he could. And kept off the trails and away from Jap patrols and cut straight to friendly lines, which were a good two days away. And he'd still be out there. Or, at least, his bones would be, because the Canal ain't nothing but cliffs and ridges and rivers and saw grass all tangled up with jungle and poisonous snakes and plants that are even worse, so you ain't going nowhere if you don't go by trail. The only thing was, the other people on that trail weren't exactly issuing hall passes to get by, so you weren't going nowhere by trail very far, either. Not unless you were Sergeant Grady Jackson.

"The first thing he did was, he had his men deflate the raft and bury it under a palm-tree log, like they were some kind of by-God commandos, or something. Then he had one of the men grab the radio, and instead of bushwhacking through the jungle toward the American side of the island, he went inland until he found a trail that angled off at a diagonal. Come midnight, they had made it to the top of a little hill without running into any Japs. That's where he set up the radio and began broadcasting in pig latin, just like it was some kind of secret code."

The old guy pulled a piece of paper from his wallet. I gathered he had carried it around for forty years as a reminder of . . . something. Printed on the paper in block letters just the way I imagined a radio message would look was:

EDRAY EAMTAY ANDEDLAY ESTIMATAY ARRIVALAY UERIL-LAGAY OMMANDCAY EETINGMAY EVENTY-EIGHTSAY OINTPAY OHAY OWTAY EETHRAY

Followed by the English translation:

244

RED TEAM LANDED ESTIMATE ARRIVAL GUERILLA COMMAND
MEETING SEVENTY-EIGHT POINT OH TWO THREE

"If it wasn't in code, the Japs never would have believed any of it."
The old man laughed.

"They would figure that pig latin out in about ten seconds." I didn't
want to be a wet blanket, but this whole thing was starting to sound
a lot like the search for Queen Inanna's waters of life.

"Actually, it took them more like eighteen hours. A marine patrol
found the documents in an abandoned command bunker a couple of
months later." The old man smiled at his memories.

"Grady and his men hid the rest of the night off the trail and all
day the next day to give the Japs plenty of time to work it out. It was
still a close thing, though. All the Japs ever had to do was just go
shoot them, like they did everybody else who washed up on their
beaches. But, once they cracked that code, they had a more elegant
idea. If they stepped out of the way, they could follow the Americans
right to the Unified Guerilla Command and bag everybody at the same
time.

"Of course they could have shot them anyway and gone on to
Possum Point by themselves, like Grady broadcast the next midnight.
Or Blue Hill, or Boot's Lick, if they could ever figure out where those
places were." The old guy laughed.

"On the fourth night Grady and his men were hungry and blistered
and bug-bit like you would not believe, but the trail had sidled up to
within a couple of klics of friendly lines, so Grady put enough real-
life info into his broadcast to send the Japs chasing off the wrong way
while he and his men haul-assed due south until they ran into concertina
wire and yelled for help.

"Nobody inside the wire was going to fall for a trick like that. They
knew there weren't any friendlies out front, and they made them wait
outside while a colonel in Intelligence came and let them in. Turned
out he'd been listening to the transmissions, too, and was delighted at
the whole idea of some kind of Unified Guerilla Command operating

behind enemy lines. When he found out Grady had made the whole thing up, he was so disappointed the son of a bitch almost threw them all back. It took the army two and a half years to get over it enough to pin that DSC on Grady.

"That was Grady Jackson's talent, making up stories other people wanted to believe."

48

I T RAINED ALL day a couple of days later when I drove to Neahkahnie Mountain. It wasn't a hard rain, but it was steady. That was the trip my wipers gave out in the Coast Range.

Every time a logging truck slammed by, a tsunami of mud and gravel would wash over my car and I'd have to reach out the window and smear the mud around the windshield so I could see. It was a relief to finally get to Grady's.

When I pulled into his driveway, it might have been drizzling for years. Maybe since the end of the last ice age. Shovels and picks were leaning against the side of the house, just as they had been every time I'd ever been there. The gas-powered generator was where it always was, and the hose coiled next to the electric pump had the grassy, overgrown look of something that had lain on the same patch of lawn too long. The branches that covered the backhoe were black and slick, most of the needles had fallen off, and the backhoe had taken on the shabby, tumbled-down look of a piece of equipment abandoned in the woods.

I treated that place like King Tut's Tomb. I didn't want anybody coming to me for answers I didn't have, and before I began the formal inventory, I photographed everything. Since then, I've gone over those photos with a magnifying glass trying to discover what I missed. But, search as I might, they always just look like pictures of Grady's stuff.

In the photographs, the ropes are coiled on the kitchen counters just the way they were coiled the Saturday I first visited. Lamps and batteries are still in the cabinets, looking as if no one ever touched them. Trowels and rock hammers are strewn across the sideboard in the room the architect meant for formal dining, and the compasses and metal detectors and the power tools that operated silently from a battery in a backpack are where they always were. Without Grady there to weave his loopy magic, it all just looked like stuff left over from somebody's life.

Before I rolled them up, the topographical maps and charts and geological surveys were still held down with Bibles and handguns, and the same enormous map was still covered with red X's showing where other diggers had come up short. The map with the mysterious markings Grady would not talk about was there, too. I studied it off and on all afternoon, but I couldn't make anything of it. Then I laid it on the floor and photographed it in sections.

There were other things in the house, of course. I found his Distinguished Service Cross, along with an eight-by-ten glossy of a young, fit Grady Jackson in an army uniform standing next to an elegant Arab in black robes with white trim who might well have been King Abdul Aziz ibn Saud of Saudi Arabia. Why Grady hadn't mentioned that picture while we were squabbling with the county was just one more thing I never figured out.

The DSC was in a cheap, dime-store frame shoved in the back of a drawer along with a citation typed on the stationery of the secretary of war. The medal didn't look like much. It had turned black over the years and was dull and unimpressive, unless you knew what it was. If you did know, it was impressive, indeed.

The citation was signed by Henry Lewis Stimson, the secretary of war, himself. Across the bottom, somebody had written in black ink:

Anksthay ofay ayay Atefulgray Ationay

It took me a while to realize that was pig latin: "Thanks of a Grateful Nation." I can't imagine Henry Lewis Stimson, secretary of war, writing something like that, but who can tell?

The gold chain was in the desk, right back where Grady had brushed it the night I stayed there. And where it had been when the troopers had confiscated it.

Grady's overalls and plaid shirts were in the bedroom closet. But he also had a linen closet filled with silk sheets and damask tablecloths he hadn't brought out the night I'd stayed with him. He had other things upstairs where he hadn't taken me. An ornate sterling punch bowl that was so big it had twenty-four silver cups hanging from the rim. His Tiffany lamps were signed, and some of his handguns turned out to be real collector's items. He had a big, jade Buddha and carved masks from Peru and Mali and Thailand. The Peruvian masks looked pre-Columbian, and the ones from Mali and Thailand looked expensive. He had a medieval Saracen helmet with a spike on top and chain mail flowing down the back, antique glassware, and a whole inventory of other things it took me days to assemble. The crazy old man in the plaid shirt and the beat-up khaki pants had lived a life of secret ostentation.

I also found a receipt for a $23,000, eight-week luxury cruise around the islands of the South Pacific, along with a first-class ticket to Singapore the following January to meet up with the ship. Whatever I had imagined about the parts of Grady's life I didn't know, I had not pictured him lounging on the deck of a cruise ship in Polynesia.

And, that wasn't the only cruise. He had a drawer filled with special offers the cruise lines had sent because he spent so much money with them. As far as I could tell, he had taken an eight- or ten-week cruise every January and February since 1972.

Which brought up another question. January and February were the months he spent with his sister in Tucson. As she was his closest heir— at least the closest heir I knew about—I needed to contact her to find out what she wanted to do with the property, but I couldn't locate her number. There were plenty of women in Grady's address books. But none from Tucson.

He had a lot of letters bundled in shoeboxes and I went through every one, letter by letter, trying to find something on his sister. As far as I could tell, Grady had saved every piece of correspondence he'd ever received. Most were from women, and they were charming and witty and made me feel homesick to know those ladies myself. From their letters, they all seemed smart and sweet and not one bit crazy. And, they treated Grady as if he were smart and charming, and not crazy, either. One was a professor of ancient Middle Eastern religions at the University of Adelaide in Australia. It all seemed very un-Grady-like, somehow.

Some of the letters came with pictures. There was a graceful, Oriental woman tucked into an envelope with Hong Kong stationery. He had a pretty Polynesian lady from Waikiki, a sweet fräulein in Berlin Town, and somebody in Barrow, Alaska, who may well have been a cute little Eskimo. For a guy who spent most of his life as a crazy man, Grady Jackson had been a regular Rick Nelson when he was traveling. But there wasn't a single letter in there from anybody who could possibly have been a sister in Tucson. In the end, I couldn't help thinking that the only sister Grady ever had was the pig-latin kind of sister who gave him an excuse to be out of town for a couple of months every winter, and to come back with a tan.

He had kept up with his army buddies, of course. There were quite a few letters of thanks, but not just for saving their lives on Guadalcanal. He'd spotted one the down payment on a house, sent both daughters of another to expensive, private colleges, and given a third enough to go into business. As far as I could tell, none of these were loans, and nobody ever paid him back.

Other than that, I couldn't find any record of a financial life. Not a single bank statement. No safe-deposit boxes. No payments from a pension fund. Not even an old income-tax form. And no mother lode of Spanish treasure, either. The coroner had pulled a small wad of twenties from the pocket of the flannel shirt he had been wearing when the postman found him, and I found a slightly larger, small wad of twenties in his sock drawer. But that was it. I could not believe—and I still do not believe, for that matter—that Grady Jackson timed his stroke to coincide with running out of whatever he lived on. But, whatever it was, I never came across it.

As far as I could make out, Grady had lived a life of private luxury. He had financed top-of-the-line cruises for himself every year, while maintaining an expensive, ongoing legal battle with the State of Oregon and, then, with Siletz County. He'd had no assets other than the goods in his house he seemed to buy as the whim hit him, no source of income, no treasure other than a gold chain he'd gotten from the king of Arabia. He hadn't even had a treasure hunt, except the one he constantly pretended to be on. Yet, he was a lavish friend and generous patron and soft touch to his army buddies.

After I got back to the office, I had a detective run a search in Flat Lick, then in eastern Kentucky, and finally over the whole state, but I never turned up any relatives of Grady's. It was like trying to find his sister. When you really looked, there wasn't anybody there. It made me wonder whether he'd actually come from Kentucky.

It did something else, too. It meant that I couldn't find any heirs. So, in the end, everything at Grady's house, the backhoe and the generator, the waterlogged piles of wooden shoring, the Saracen helmet and damask tablecloths and silk sheets, the rusty shovels, the flannel shirts in his closet, the ropes coiled on his kitchen counters, the batteries in his cabinets, the Bibles, the guns, the roll of twenties the coroner found in his pocket, and, most of all, the gold chain we had worked so hard to get back, all escheated to the State of Oregon.

49

E VERYTHING I DID for Grady came full circle, and none of it amounted
to much of anything. I should have listened to Thaddeus. "Most
things," he told me the night he died, "blow over."

What's a mentor for, if you can't learn from him? But I was young,
and headstrong, and didn't give his wisdom the respect it was due and
wasted a lot of needless adrenaline stewing over whether I had a conflict
of interest with Grady, and what the grand jury had in mind for me,
and if the Motel Lady was going to show up at the hearing, and how
to get Abby out of going to jail for the rest of her life, none of which
would have cost Thaddeus Silk any sleep at all.

Even twenty-some years later, I still lose sleep over what might be.
And worry and struggle to make things happen and, often as not, don't
add any more to the result than if I had been trying to make things
come out the other way. The truth is, you can't control how your parts
are fitted together, and Thaddeus Silk . . . well, in a lot of ways, the
workmanship on Thaddeus Silk was more comfortable than mine is
on me.

I shouldn't have worried about Abby's case. Ten days before *The
State of Oregon v. Abby Birdsong* was scheduled to be tried, the
Sorrowful DA dropped the charges. The sheriff had misplaced some
key evidence, and the DA no longer felt he could prove his case. How,
exactly, an evidence room could lose track of four and a half tons of
marijuana was hard to imagine.

If it had been any other four and a half tons, the answer would
have been simple. The sheriff would have sold it. But picturing
Sheriff New Broom or anybody else unloading four and a half tons

of *Abby's* dope on the black market took more imagination than I could conjure.

Where government incompetence was concerned, though, Shelley's imagination wasn't nearly as constrained. "Of course they misplaced it." He gave me his best how-naïve-can-you-get look. "Those fools are probably wading hip-deep in Abby's shit right now trying to find the evidence tags to tell them where it is."

"I told you"—Abby began to cry at the idea of deputies wading through her private four and a half tons of shit—"it couldn't have been more than a ton and a half." To calm herself, she pulled out a little square of paper and a pinch of bad-looking marijuana and rolled a jay. When she lit up, the smoke was just as foul as the smoke that had come off the ten-year-old shit the sheriff had misplaced.

A few days later, I remembered the twenty-ninth microcassette, the tape Shelley had taken home the night we shot up the Love Nest. I'd been right. Thaddeus hadn't had anything on Shelley. It was that New Broom Son-of-a-Bitch sheriff out to make a name for himself whose voice had been on the tape—I was certain of that when I thought about it—the one who took the bribes, then wouldn't cover for the SurfSea with the tobacco Nazis.

The one Thaddeus had had to call and advocate a whole new envelope full of reasons to keep the law off their backs. The one Thaddeus had undoubtedly called from the phone on his desk attached to the tape recorder.

The same New Broom Son-of-a-Bitch sheriff whose evidence room had misplaced four and a half tons of marijuana ten days before Abby was to go to trial.

The very same New Broom Son-of-a-Bitch, I'd lay money on, who'd gotten a call from Shelley just before all the dope went missing.

50

THE WEEK BEFORE Christmas, Queen Inanna came to visit. Her full name was Dr. Claudia Elfin Anna Toutant de la Courte Morgan. She was professor emerita of Ancient Middle Eastern religions at the University of Adelaide, and she was staying at the Benson Hotel.

She'd had six older brothers, and when she was born, her daddy had been so delighted to have a little girl he insisted on the Elfin Anna part and had still called her that years later in front of her students. Grady had called her Elf Inanna, and then, after she turned down his marriage proposal, he promoted her to Queen. Sometimes, she said, she called him Dumuzi. I called her Claudia. We talked about the names over supper at Jake's.

I had written her, and the other ladies Grady had been corresponding with, when he'd died. Most sent back polite notes, but Claudia had called from Australia to tell me that she was planning to speak at a conference on Sumerian mythology at Reed College. She got a lot of invitations for that sort of thing, but she had accepted the one in Portland so she could spend some time with Grady. She still planned to go through with the trip.

The very idea that Grady had a lady friend was so out of context with anything I remembered about him, it would have been enough to make me want to get together with her. But Claudia sounded so elegant on the phone, and she was so charming, that it almost felt like a date when we met for dinner.

She was a slender, stylish, silver-haired lady in her late sixties, I guessed. She was poised and self-confident and funny and, while we talked, downed three dark beers and a plate of crab legs. I had never seen a woman her age do that, and I was smitten.

She told me she had fallen in love with Grady on a sailing yacht cruising the Great Barrier Reef. Since then, they had cruised together every year she wasn't teaching summer quarter, which, when I thought about it, fell in January and February in Australia.

The Grady she had taken those cruises with was urbane and witty and comfortable with rich people and university people both. Women adored him, she told me. He had been generous with his time, and his concern, and filled with stories. He'd had elegant taste in wine and been at home in every city in East Asia the cruise ships visited. Once, in Kuala Lumpur, he had shown her how to buy ivory. Another time, in Colombo, he taught her to haggle for raw jewels. But the interesting part, in her mind, was how Grady handled himself. He never raised his voice. He never acted anxious or said anything inappropriate, even in the most high-pressure situations. He was, she told me, a tribute to the kind of gentleman a man could be. The man she had known on her cruises was definitely not the Grady Jackson I had known.

But he was. I still had the records of the cruises—boxed up along with everything else he'd owned—waiting for the State of Oregon to come take them away once the statutory time had passed and no relatives had showed up. I checked, and Grady had been in Kuala Lumpur in January of 1977. "When that President Jimmy of yours took office," as Claudia remembered it. Grady had been on the cruise to Sri Lanka the January she toured the gem stores in Colombo. And he had been in Singapore and Bali and Cebu City, all just as she remembered.

She wanted me to take her to Neahkahnie Mountain. Grady had told her so many stories about the funny old crank who spent his life up there looking for Spanish gold that she wanted to meet him for herself. I told her I was sorry, but the crank hadn't been seen for a while, so I couldn't introduce them. But I remembered him well and told her some stories of my own about the old fellow.

"He asked me to marry him, you know," she said.

I could see why. I'd only known her a few minutes, but, already, I was beginning to regret that I wasn't in my late sixties and in a position to come courting, myself.

"It wouldn't have worked. I wasn't going to leave my situation at the university, and, well, Grady, he had . . . not that he wasn't willing to move to Adelaide. He didn't have to work, once he brought all that silver out of China. And, except for his sister, he didn't have any family, so he convinced himself he would be perfectly happy picking up stakes and joining me, but I couldn't see it. I knew him too well."

"Sister?" I asked, thinking of the sister I'd never been able to track down. "The one in Tucson?"

"I don't think so. He told me she lived in Hong Kong. She'd married a Chinese banker, and it was his contacts on the mainland that set up that silver deal. I'm surprised Grady didn't mention that." She laughed. And, then, started telling me the same story the swindler had been telling drunks at the SurfSea the night Grady had plugged him. "Are you sure he didn't tell you this?"

I shook my head.

She smiled to herself at the thought of Grady showing up in Red China with a string of mules to buy price-controlled Communist silver to carry back and sell on the free market. "It was all on the up and up, but, still, nobody wanted to get caught in the People's Republic with a mule train of silver. And it became pretty clear somebody was keeping a close eye on him when he started back to Hong Kong. He figured it was the Chinese government, and they were going to murder him for the silver and claim he was a spy. I think they would have, too, but they didn't know Grady Jackson. He had a radio, and he started broadcasting to somebody named Morning Flower, who was waiting at the Hong Kong border to smuggle him and the silver across to freedom. So, instead of murdering him on the road, the authorities decided to wait at the border. That way they could get him, the silver, and the entire Morning Flower smuggling ring at the same time. But they never did. The night they planned to spring the trap, Grady was on the other side of the Pearl River estuary in Macao, along with the entire shipment of silver and the speedboat he'd bribed out of an official in Dongguan. Marrying a man like that . . ." She smiled to herself, again, at the memory of Grady. "It never would have worked. He had all those other women friends, and I . . . well, I just told him I was Queen Inanna, and there was something to that. I had a few gentlemen friends of my own . . ."

"He talked about Queen Inanna sometimes," I told her. "He said how unfaithful she was to her lovers." Then: "You're the one who told him about her?"

"That's my area of specialty," she said quietly, then sipped at her beer.

"It's a strange business to modern ears," I replied, thinking of the naked body hanging on Ereshkigal's wall.

"I'm surprised he would have told you that." Then she blushed, realizing I hadn't mentioned anything revealing.

Then, knowing the cat was pretty much out of the bag, she smiled and told me, "You have to remember, he was the most charming man, and, well, I was somewhat of an authority on Queen Inanna and I did want to make it up to him for not marrying him. When we tied up in Padang, I went into the market and bought a lot of cheap jewelry, and that evening we set up seven little gates around our stateroom . . ." She ground to a halt, lost in what she and Grady had done.

That conversation over dinner was the only real glimpse I ever had into Grady's life away from Neahkahnie Mountain. And it wasn't any easier to piece together than the part I had known. Some things I'm pretty sure of, though. Except for the pig-latin kind, Grady didn't have a sister in Hong Kong any more than he'd had a sister in Tucson. And he never smuggled any silver out of Red China. I checked his passport. He was never in Macao, and the only time he was in Hong Kong was years later on the cruise with Claudia. It's pretty easy to see where that story came from, though.

In the end, it wasn't that Grady walked a line that looped in and out between sanity and lunacy, it was that the line looped between his life as a witty, charming world traveler, and his life as the Crazy Man of Neahkahnie Mountain. And the things he learned in one part of his life, he translated into the things he needed in the other.

The elegant, stylish Queen Inanna he cruised the world with turned into the focus of his insanity back home, while the finest thing he had done in the life I knew, eluding the Japanese for four days on Guadalcanal, mixed together with a man he shot in a bar and transmogrified in his other life into an excuse for being rich. I was beginning to see how Grady worked it. What I couldn't figure out was why?

51

A FEW DAYS before we closed Thaddeus's office for good, the police finally located the ancient, Spanish treasure the DA had needed to convict Grady. They came across it in a pawnshop. Jolene was reading a biography of Nikola Tesla when the detective came by with the photos.

"Recognize these?" He handed me an envelope with eight-by-ten glossies. "We found them at the Happy Hocker."

"No." I shook my head as I shuffled through the photos. "I never saw any of this stuff before."

It must have been a surprise to find something that nice in a pawnshop. They were pictures of gold bracelets and rings, a couple of other rings set with red stones that could have been rubies, and a gold crucifix that looked like something a Spanish aristocrat might have worn or, when I thought about it, the pope. I had absolutely no motive to tell the police, or anybody else, that they looked familiar.

"We think they're Spanish," the detective told me. He was a middle-aged black man with a spectacular potbelly. "We don't need you to identify them. Ms. Silk has already done that. We just thought you might know something. Actually"—the detective paused—"we had a little wager on it. I've got a pair of Beavers tickets riding on the fact that you recognize them."

"Well, then"—I laughed—"looks like you lose."

"Looks like." He smiled a rueful smile. "But those pictures aren't really why I'm here. I'm here to find out what happened to that gold brooch with the huge emerald Ms. Silk keeps calling us about. The pawnbroker claims he never saw it. Know anything?"

"No." I shook my head, again. "I can't say I—"

"Pity," he interrupted. "We were hoping to put an end to those calls. Mind if I have a look around?"

"Okay by me." By then, Thaddeus's office had been pawed through by every law-enforcement official in two counties. But he didn't go into Thaddeus's office. He went into mine.

Whoa, I thought. "What are you looking for in there?"

"Brooch, maybe." He shrugged. "Pawn tickets. Things like that. You told me I could look around."

"Not in my office, I didn't," I said as I followed him in. "If you want to look in *my* office, you're going to have to come back with a warrant."

"Hot damn, bro." He raised his hand in a high five. "You just won me a dinner for two at the Ringside. We got these rookies down at the station said you might actually let me look around. Kids can be so naïve these days, that's the problem with this matriarchal society we live in. A child can grow big enough to look like an adult and never know the first thing about the way the world works." That downtown police station was beginning to sound like a gambling den.

"I'll just be going now." He grinned as he walked over to the door. "See if I can rustle me up a warrant. Now in the meantime, no matter how much money you owe that fancy lawyer of yours, don't you go trying to unload that brooch, too. We got all the pawnshops covered." He opened the door to leave, then turned back to me.

"About that other bet." He winked. "I never claimed you would identify that stuff in the Happy Hocker. Like I say, Ms. Silk already did that. The only thing I bet was that you would recognize it." He paused to let what he was about to say sink in. "I think you did, too."

I think the police must have known they were on the losing side by then, because nobody ever came by with a warrant.

52

THE NEXT MORNING, Abby Birdsong walked into the office and demanded her half of Grady's hoard of twenties. Shelley came with her, to help carry it away.

"It's my money," she said in a small voice, invoking the universal law of dibs. "I saw it first after Grady." She pulled out a rag and dabbed at her eyes. "I was out there on the beach and I saw the money and—"

"Money?" I must have sounded baffled.

"I told you. That night we were in the dunes and the *federales* blew away those drug runners and we ran over and found the dope and . . ." She sniffed, again.

"Only . . . only I don't think it was *federales*. There was just this one person doing the shooting and he was up the beach by that hole Grady dug to look for treasure. He was cool about it and let them unload the whole boatful of dope onto the beach, and it wasn't until one of them started heading back toward the boat carrying a big, square bale of something that Grady nailed him and he crumpled into the surf. Then Grady got another one, and the last two made a run for it, and he cut one of them down before they'd gotten ten feet, but the other guy dove in the boat and gunned it in reverse and took off in the darkness. Grady took some shots at him, but I'm not sure he hit anything. Anyway, the sound of the motor kept heading out to sea until it was—"

"Grady?" I asked. "Grady Jackson?"

She nodded.

"You are telling me"—I leaned forward in amazement—"that Grady Jackson sat in that hole of his and blew away four—"

263

"Well, I'm not sure about *sat*." She sniffled. "The hole was pretty deep. And I think he only got three. But Grady had a rifle out there and he was practically living in his hole by then to keep poachers away. And there weren't any *federales*, that's for sure, because the phone down at the SurfSea was busted, so they never got the call about that dope drop. Besides," she said slowly, "I saw Grady Jackson." She sounded positive about that. "Me and Shelley, we both saw him. You tell him, Shelley."

"It was Grady, alright." Shelley nodded, then went back to thumbing through one of my constitutional-law books, checking for loopholes.

"Like I told you, we were lying in the dune grass, and when the shooting stops, Grady walks over and kicks the bodies. Then he went and found the bale that dead guy dropped and tried to roll it up onto the sand, but it had gotten wet and a lot of it broke off. It took Grady a long time to toss the pieces up on the beach. When he had them all safe from washing away, he dragged the dead guy up, too."

I was hoping there wouldn't turn out to be a fourth version of this story in which Abby Birdsong was the one who pulled the trigger.

"Then Grady fired up that backhoe of his and started scooping out a new hole, not more than thirty feet from where he was digging for treasure. By then, all I wanted was to get out of there, but Shelley told me shussssh, and we just lay in the grass while Grady buried those three guys."

Motel Lady had been right about Grady running a backhoe on the beach that night. The neighbors who'd complained to the state had been right, too. Only, Grady hadn't been digging for buried treasure, as they all thought.

"I don't know how long we waited, I never was that scared before. Anyway, the time finally came when he finished up with the backhoe. Then he went over to the place where the boat had been and picked up the biggest chunk of the bale the dead guy had dropped and carried it off down the beach until we couldn't see him in the dark. Big as Grady was, he had trouble with it.

"Once we couldn't see him anymore, Shelley went over to check out the stack of dope, didn't you, babe? And I went to see what that dead guy had been carrying to the boat that was so important Grady killed those people over it. When I got to where the boat had been, I stepped on something that made a rustly sound. At first, I thought it was seaweed, but when I picked it up, it wasn't seaweed at all. The tide was going out and the beach was covered with these bundles of twenty-dollar bills. Each one was about an inch thick, and they were all wet and sandy from rolling around in the surf, and there were hundreds of them, and that wasn't even counting that most of them were in the bale Grady had hauled off.

Motel Lady was right about that, too. Grady really had lugged something big and square off the beach. Only, she'd been wrong about the rotting chest. What she'd seen him set down next to his car was a sandy, wet bale of twenty-dollar bills. No wonder it was so heavy. And, no wonder it fell apart and he had to crawl around in the dark scooping handfuls into the trunk.

"I threw the bundle of twenties down and got out of there," Abby went on. "There was no way I was going to keep something like that. Whoever was out there in the ocean waiting for the boat Grady had been shooting at, he was going to come looking for that money, and three dead people were enough, without including me and Shelley on the list, and . . . All I wanted was to get off the beach, but when I got back to the dunes, Shelley was loading the dope into Susie B. The funny part was, he doesn't even smoke the stuff. He just liked the idea of slipping it in under the nose of Mr. Whiskers, and you know Shelley. It was easier to help him finish loading than to argue over it."

"Man in Whiskers." Shelley looked up from the book on constitutional law. "Mr. Whiskers is a cat-food commercial."

"We weren't half-done," Abby picked back up, "before Grady shows up with a garbage bag, and we had to lay down in the grass again while he scooped up bundles of twenties. After he finally left, we finished loading the dope and were out of there. I don't know if he came back or not."

I wondered whether Grady ever figured out that Abby and Shelley had been there that night. He must have known something was up when he didn't hear anything about tons of marijuana showing up on the beach the next morning. Whatever, he lucked out. No marijuana meant no questions. At least, that's how I saw it at the time. Now, it seems a lot more likely that Abby and Shelley were in on it from the beginning.

Regardless of what the arrangements really were, they had pulled off the perfect crime. Grady had gotten rich, and Abby had driven away with a truckful of primo, at least for a while, Panamanian weed. The only people who knew something was missing were the real owners, and they weren't going to come looking for it because they thought the Feds had it.

And the Feds didn't know anything had happened. At least, that's what Abby and Shelley thought. But, after that meeting with the DEA lady, I'm not so sure. Maybe the Feds were just happy to have the drug runners blown away, no matter who did it, and were glad not to be involved.

Whatever, all Grady and Abby had to do was just lie low, which she had done a good job of until I blew her cover on that radio show. Grady had done an even better job. He lay low right in plain sight. There was no way he could turn up suddenly rich without attracting the attention of some pissed-off drug dealers, so he turned up crazy, instead. But crazy with a gold chain to flash around in case he needed to have his treasure hunt taken seriously.

As a legal proposition, I'm not sure dibs rises to the level of an enforceable right. And I am not going to go into whether Abby and I worked out some kind of arrangement or, if we did, what it was. But, even if we did, it didn't make any difference, because we never found the twenties. When we couldn't locate them at Grady's house, we pored over the pictures I'd taken when I was inventorying his estate. Then, I had a blueprint company assemble the photos of the map with the mysterious markings into a new map sixty inches by forty-eight, and we went over that, too, and still came up empty-handed. Which only made sense, when I thought about it. The state patrol had searched

Grady's house and hadn't come up with anything but the chain. The twenties weren't easy to find.

We trudged over Neahkahnie Mountain until I located the shored-up excavation Grady and I had passed the day he'd showed me around up there. It still looked solid and seemed newer than I remembered, so that might mean something. But, by the time we found it, it had been months since Grady had died. It had rained almost every day since then, and we couldn't tell whether the hole had recently been worked or not. So, in the end, Grady kept his secret safe from us, just as he had from everybody else.

The whole thing had been a setup from the beginning, I'm almost certain about that. Grady had known about the drug runners, everybody at the SurfSea knew. He hadn't left bartending to go treasure hunting, he went treasure hunting to have an excuse to wait on the beach with a backhoe and a rifle at a place he knew drug runners were bound to show up.

When the night came, jimmying the phone would have been easy. The SurfSea was still his bar. And, bringing Abby and Shelley in on the deal would have been smart. It kept the marijuana from being discovered, which is the only way he could be sure the rest of the plan would work.

One of the hardest things a man can ever do is let himself look like a fool. But that's how Grady played it, spending his life on a crackpot treasure hunt everybody laughed at. In return, he gained privacy and held on to his twenties. As far as I know, he was never pestered by hustlers or newly surfaced relatives wanting a piece of the action or burglars or, even, tax collectors. In a world obsessed by celebrity, Grady Jackson had peace and security and, even, a measure of notoriety. But, only a measure. Nobody thought he was strange enough, or interesting enough, to bother much about. And, not to put too fine a point on it, for a person like Grady, it must have been fun weaving endless, lunatic fantasies about himself. Grady Jackson's bargain was not the bargain of a fool.

It wasn't until I thought about those army buddies of his, and the private ceremony they'd held at Neahkahnie Mountain after the interment in Portland, that I realized where the money went. If Grady ever told anybody about the twenties, those would have been the guys. And they were alone over there two days before I went to take inventory.

Something else I realized was that, as long as they kept their mouths shut, it was too late for me or Abby or the tax man or the probate court or any damn body else to do anything about it.

The only thing I couldn't figure was where the brooch and the rest of the treasure in Thaddeus's safe had come from. It took me nineteen years from the time we closed the doors on Thaddeus Silk and Assoc. to get to the bottom of that, if I ever did.

53

THE DAY WE closed the office, Jolene's papers finally showed up.
Keeping her out of jail should have been easy. I needed to mail
the documents Thaddeus had already filled out, then wait for the state
to get back to me. I think if the documents had been filled out by
anybody else, that's probably the way it would have worked. But having
Thaddeus's name involved almost brought the process to a complete
halt. In the end, the state dragged its feet and argued every little point
and burned up a huge amount of lawyer time that would have been
worth something if my time had been worth anything at all, just then.
They even sent an investigator around to check up on us, and he didn't
need to talk to Jolene long to realize she didn't have any business being
in custody. He filled out his report, and the morning we closed the
office, the papers confirming she was a free woman finally arrived.

I called her into my office and showed her where to sign. Then I
signed and put the papers into an envelope to mail back to the state.
When that was taken care of, I handed her a letter of recommenda-
tion. It was more glowing than strictly accorded with the facts, and I
hoped it would do her some good.

I had never planned to ask for a fee, but when she offered to pay,
I was tempted. "Here." She dropped something heavy and soft into
my hand. "I'm hoping . . ." She lowered her eyes. "I don't have much
cash, and I was hoping this will . . ."

This turned out to be a folded bit of black velvet. Inside was a gold
brooch with a medium-size uncut emerald in the center. The brooch
was beautifully filigreed and, on the back, was flowing, Arabic script.

It was exactly the kind of thing that could have lain hidden on

Neahkahnie Mountain, or under the sand, or in the water just offshore, for four hundred years—exactly the kind of delicate, Middle Eastern craftsmanship to make its way down the Persian Gulf to Calicut, then through the Indian Ocean and on to Manila, to be sold to a Spanish merchant for Inca silver. All of a sudden, I knew what had happened to the treasure in Thaddeus's safe.

Jolene had taken it. She knew where Thaddeus kept the combination. Everybody but Sophie knew. Keeping the combination out of his sister's hands was what let Thaddeus keep the bourbon in the safe. Somehow, during the confusion with Sophie calling the television stations and making a hubbub the morning Thaddeus died, Jolene had cleaned out the treasure. When I thought about it, she had been a more experienced shoplifter than I'd given her credit for.

As a theoretical matter, I could have hung on to that brooch, I suppose. Jolene paid me with it and she expected me to keep it, which meant I came by it honestly. And, it seemed to me that she had at least as good a claim on it as Sophie. Better, I thought. The way Thaddeus had ripped her off, that brooch was just part of what he owed her. So, as an abstract legal proposition, I didn't have any trouble accepting the brooch as a fee.

As a practical matter, though, I wasn't going to touch it. I had been in the office the day that brooch, and a lot of other treasure, disappeared. I had known where the combination was, too, and I did not want to have to explain to the Bar Association, or the district attorney, how I hadn't stolen the brooch myself, but had only accepted it from the convicted felon in the office who did steal it. So, I did the honorable thing. I handed it back.

Jolene folded the velvet around the brooch and gave me a shy smile and walked back to the reception area. I don't think she was used to people cutting her breaks.

Before we went home that afternoon, something else occurred to me and I called her back into my office. Maybe, I thought, she knew more about where Thaddeus had gotten the treasure than she'd let on. But, when I asked her who Engine Joe was, she just shook her head. I wasn't really surprised. I'd been pretty sure she wouldn't know.

After we shut the office, I kept a copy of Thaddeus's client list. I figured it was a good place to go prospecting for new business. I also figured that Engine Joe's real name was on that list and, given time, I could puzzle it out.

But I never could. I must have gone over those names a hundred times and made dozens of calls before I was ready to admit that, whoever Engine Joe was, I wasn't going to find him that way.

54

I ONLY SAW Jolene once after that, at Tail Pipe's funeral. They married a few months after we closed the office, and he died a couple of years later, from his wounds and liver failure. Jolene said it was pretty bad at the end.

The Veterans Administration buried him up at Willamette National Cemetery, no more than a hundred yards from Grady. It was a sad little funeral, and they didn't even play taps. Tail Pipe didn't rate a bugler, and the tape recorder had broken.

Abby and Pink Milk Shake and Ropy Arms would all be pushing seventy now, as hard as that is to imagine. In my mind's eye, they're holed up in a storage locker nobody ever mentioned to me, filled with rotting marijuana from a return trip to the beach thirty-five years ago nobody ever mentioned, either. I don't know what became of Shelley. I always thought I might hear something about him, but I never did.

Ten years ago, Sophie Silk surfaced, briefly, as the oldest, and probably loudest, person ever charged with violating Oregon's security laws, when she tried to sell shares in a treasure-hunting corporation on Neahkahnie Mountain. Nothing ever came of it, though, and she was never tried. She must be in her late eighties, now, if she's alive at all.

I grew older, too, somehow. I was still lucky and I kept winning more than I lost, although, to give me my due, I had some spectacular crashes and burns along the way. My practice never made much money, though, and in the late eighties when I wrote a book about my experiences in Vietnam, I discovered a way of going broke that was a lot more satisfying than law, and I closed up my own shop and turned into a writer and never looked back.

Somewhere along there, I went through a practice marriage. I would feel a lot worse about that except my wife was practicing, too. After we split, she practiced on three more guys, but I never heard she got it right.

The Sorrowful DA got the job at the Department of Justice, even though he never did figure out where the treasure was coming from. Years later, when a new attorney general came into power, the Sorrowful Now Deputy Attorney General bought a vineyard near Amity, took early retirement, and, the last I heard, was pouring sips of wine to tourists in a tasting room off Highway 99 West.

The old judge in Siletz County held on for a few years, then, one day, just stopped coming to work. His clerk said he'd lost patience with the Court of Appeals looking over his shoulder.

I wish I could say it was Judge Wobberly's seat Lydia Stonemason filled when they put her on the court, but it wasn't. She kept soldiering on in her foggy way, making a hash of every carefully thought-out estate plan that came before her until she died at her desk in 1995.

Lydia spent her judicial career confounding politicians who wanted her to carry out their agenda on higher courts, and attorneys who imagined those same higher courts might overturn one of her rulings. During her time on the bench, she turned down two Democratic governors who approached her about serving on the state supreme court. She told them she liked people too much to give up being a trial judge, which is the same thing she told President Reagan and, a few years later, President Bush Sr., when they asked her about the Ninth Circuit Court of Appeals.

Of all the people I knew when I was starting out, she was the one I stayed closest to. Even though I had trouble with her bill, I paid it, somehow, and for the next almost two decades, she remained a guide and an ally and a friend.

One afternoon, after I had lost a particularly unpleasant jury trial in her court involving accountants testifying in way-too-much detail about what the dirt in dump trucks was worth, she summoned me into chambers and introduced me to her clerk. It took me about five seconds to realize I had just met the woman who was going to be my real wife, but, as Lydia put it, sometimes I can be a bit slow. Three months later, back in those same chambers, Judge Lydia Stonemason presiding, the court stenographer and the bailiff witnessing, her clerk and I became a legal couple.

Over the years, Lydia's hair turned white, and her features softened, but she stayed as straight and her eyes as blue and as clear as they had been when I'd first walked into her office. Then, as her sixty-fifth birthday approached, she announced her retirement.

The judges threw quite a party for her. She gave a little speech that wound up with her mentioning how she and Hal had wanted to move to Aruba ever since they had visited the Caribbean on their honeymoon.

When she sat down, one of the senior judges banged on a glass with a large, bone-handled hunting knife. "Attention," he said. And he got it. "A man is still allowed to carry one of these in here, I see." The rest of us laughed. *Here* was the main ballroom in the oldest, fanciest, most exclusive, and, therefore, most lawyer-infested country club in the state, with its own golf course and several hundred yards of manicured riverfront on the Willamette south of town. The judge who banged the glass was a life member of the National Rifle Association, contributed to all sorts of Second Amendment causes, and his struggles with the county ordinance making it a felony to carry a weapon into the courthouse were the stuff of cocktail-party legend.

Whether he had actually lost that struggle was a matter of considerable rumor in legal circles. Plenty of lawyers had noticed that, when he showed up at the courthouse, the deputy on duty always seemed to fiddle with the controls on the metal detector before he walked through. And that, coincidentally, a number of other court employees and judges who were known to support the right to keep and bear arms seemed to walk through at the same time.

He gestured to the back of the room, and a clerk began to make his way through the crowd. When we saw the clerk was carrying a huge cherrywood plaque, the lawyers and judges in the room began to clap and cheer. Bolted to the plaque was a big, steel circular-saw blade, with the words:

Fourteenth Occasional Rip-Saw Award
presented to
Lydia Averet Stonemason, Circuit Judge

In recognition of her outstanding achievement in never backing down from the superlatives the Legal Community holds dear, to wit:

For having served eighteen years as a trial judge without being overturned on appeal

On the event of her much-envied retirement, December 29, 2000

The Occasional Rip-Saw was not a formal honor. Nobody was supposed to know who gave it, or how the recipients were chosen, but it was old and prestigious and only went to lawyers and judges with an absolutely unblemished record in some regard, which meant it wasn't given often. Getting Rip-Sawed was the highest honor a member of the legal community could aspire to, even though no one in the room was ever allowed to mention it outside the room, so pretend you didn't read this.

The very first Occasional Rip-Saw went to a municipal judge who had neglected to rule for twenty-three years on the city's request to condemn the land beneath a brewery. As he put it long after he retired, and much longer after the municipal offices the city had wanted to build on the condemned land had been built somewhere else, "I like to drink beer." That had been in 1894, and only a dozen Rip-Saws had been handed out since.

Eight years before Lydia retired, the Thirteenth Occasional Rip-Saw went to a lawyer who had managed to bill 273 hours of work in a single afternoon. A lot of lawyers thought the prestige of the award had been diminished by giving it for that sort of thing. Two hundred